Holistic Christian Education Towards Transforming Indian Congregations

Christian Heritage Rediscovered

The Series, as the name suggests, is meant to focus on Christian Faith & Living vis-à-vis topics like Literature & Poetry, Indigenous Philosophizing, Ethical response towards Agriculture, Health & Healing, Science & Technology, Eco-feminist Theology, Sociological approach towards Human Rights, Law & Politics, Arts, History of Ideas, Ancient Civilizations, Cultural Contiguity, Religious Cosmologies & Mysticism, Footsteps of famous Theologians, World Peace & Harmony, Global Capitalism, Network Marketing, Cybertheology, Population & Demographics, Epigraphic Studies, Contextualized Education, and many others. We welcome a Mss. on any topic/s mentioned, whether they are original works, scholarly monographs, collections of conference papers, revised dissertations, or translations of historical documents. Through the Series we, the Publishers, are striving to put forward published works that may help Institutions, Academic Bodies, Researchers, Scholars and the World at large in furthering their respective knowledge and understanding on the concerned subject. We welcome your comments on our efforts and further suggestions on how we can foster the upcoming thought provoking theologically grounded books.

Christian Heritage Rediscovered - 76

Holistic Christian Education Towards Transforming Indian Congregations

Moses Boosa

CWI

Christian World Imprints

First Published in 2019 by

Christian World Imprints
Christian Publishing & Books from India
H-12 Bali Nagar, **New Delhi-110015**
info@christianworldimprints.com
www.ChristianWorldImprints.com
Phone: +91 11 25465925

ISBN: 978-93-5148-341-0

Cover Photo "Used with permission from SMCI".

Printed in India.

Contents

Dedication

I dedicate this research work to my father Late Mr. Joseph Boosa and mother Mrs. Shantha Boosa. My father-in-law Late Mr. G. V. Janardhan and mother-in-law Mrs. Gladys Janardhan.

Also, would like to dedicate to my dear wife Glory Arathi for always being my strength and giving me freedom to be away from home for a couple of years and to my children Alan, Merlin and Sarah without whose support I would have not completed this research study.

This book in its original form is the thesis submitted to the Senate of Serampore College (University), India, towards the degree of Master of Theology and is published with the written permission. The author is responsible for the title, content and opinions expressed in it.

The original title of the thesis is "Holistic Christian Education towards Transformation of the Congregations of Southern Methodist Churches in Telangana and Andhra Pradesh."

Foreword

I am delighted to pen a few words to this significant contribution in the area of Christian education in terms of its attempt to place the holistic Christian education in the context of transforming Indian congregations. The challenges encountered by the Indian congregations within and from 'outside' call for a multidimensional response and I strongly believe the holistic education has a vital role in it.

Holistic education is favoured in a pluralistic society such as India, by educationists and academicians, for, it could be differentiated from the education that gives importance to intellectual development alone. The holistic nurturing of individual productivity and quality Christian life are crucial components for church growth. Holistic Christian education has a great impact on the total transformation of an individual's understanding such as social, spiritual, psychological, cultural, economic, and political aspects. The author has specifically worked on the concept of holistic Christian education and contributed a good foundational understanding of how this concept helps the congregations towards holistic development.

This book, further, provides a wide variety of material which is useful for theological students as well to those who are interested in the Christian educational ministry of the church. I personally congratulate the author for his sincere efforts toward academic excellence to make Christian education relevant to the present Indian ecclesiastical context. I trust that the readers would highly be enriched by the author's insights, findings and suggestions to realize God's mission to establish God's Reign through God's people, i.e., the congregations.

Rev. Dr. A. Israel David
Faculty Dean &
Dean of Christian Ministry Department
Union Biblical Seminary

Preface

The task for Christian educators is not just to identify ways to implement change, but to create/educate congregations that are continuously adaptive to change. Few questions are to be asked 1) Can Christian educators help congregations develop a new holistic model? 2) Can the strategies that are the core abilities become an obstacle for changes in congregations? 3) In addition to this, whether these strategies help the congregations to become global, digitally, ethnically relevant in an ever-changing and diverse cultures?

The content and the methods of imparting Christian education may not be adequate for the holistic transformation of the congregations. There is an emphasis on transmission of Christian beliefs, traditions, and norms rather than holistic transformation of an individual. As a result, an individual is not enabled to be relevant in the face of contextual realities like competition in the academic levels (cognitive development), social relationships, dehumanizing situation from large sections of society, political view, cultural diversities, and ecological issues that threaten the very existence of life. The findings prove and validate the hypothesis of this research that the education ministry of SMCI is not adequately impacting the life and ministry of congregational members toward holistic transformation.

Christian education is a vital part of Christian ministry by which the church seeks to fulfill its mandate in this world. Christian education empowers people to grow to maturity and develop their full potential in order to engage in God's work in the world. With this in mind, the researcher attempts to study the objectives, and assess the importance of Holistic Christian Education toward Transformation of Congregations of the Southern Methodist Churches in Telangana & Andhra Pradesh (SMCI).

The research study has been divided into four chapters. The first chapter, presents the objectives, scope, hypothesis, methodology, definitions of keywords, and brief geographical background of Telangana and Andhra Pradesh with the history of SMCI.

The second chapter attempts to provide the literature review of the theoretical aspects such as the Biblical understanding of Christian Education, meaning, and purpose of (Holistic) Christian Education, the role of the church in the holistic transformation through Christian education.

Chapter three furnishes the analysis and interpretation of the empirical data collected from the sample group of SMCI. For the collection of data, two sets of questionnaires were administered. The researcher received responses from 140 members and 22 leaders or pastors of SMCI. The total number of respondents is 162.

Finally, chapter four concludes with research findings, suggestions and recommendations for the effective implementation of the holistic approach to Christian Education toward the complete transformation of the congregations of SMCI.

I praise God for the opportunity to do a research study on Christian education. I express my gratitude to Dr. H. G. Mithra, who guided me in the research work. A special gratitude to Rev. William Daniel of Southern Methodist Church, Dr. Muthuraj Swamy, Dr. Asish Thomas Koshy and Rev. Dr. A. Israel David for helping me to publish my research study, Dr. Wilson Paluri, Rev. Muthu John, Dr. Stanly Jones, Rev. Ch. Prem Kumar, Dr. N. Subramani, Mr. Yeshwant Bakkavemana, Rev. Sophia Makasare, Mr. Nangsonlian Ngaihte, Rev. Deepak Vara Kumar, Mr. S.P. Barnabas, Mr. Robin Jayaprakash, Mr. Mathew Covington, Mr. Simon George, Union Biblical Seminary, Oldham Methodist Church, and many other individuals for their support and help in various aspects of my research study. Most importantly, grateful to Southern Methodist Church based in Orangeburg, SC, USA.

Last but not least, it is my privilege to thank the Christian World Imprints, a renowned Christian publishing company in India who encourage many young and emerging writers to publish. I am grateful to Mr. Sudhanshu Kanda and CWI for their kindness to publish this research work.

Moses Boosa
2019

List of Figures

List of Tables

List of Abbreviations

GSDP	:	Gross State Domestic Product
IT	:	Information Technology
MCI	:	Methodist Church in India
SMC	:	Southern Methodist Church (International)
SMCI	:	Southern Methodist Church in India

Chapter 1

Introduction

Christian education is a reflective process—*information for transformation* or faith formation through lifelong learning, retrospection and introspection about ones' own family, church, society, universe, environment, and God in broader sense.[1] Christian education has made idealistic strides toward addressing the dualisms between "head knowledge" and "heart knowledge" that holistic education addresses.[2] Darcy Berube based on this holistic vision of Christian education noted that, holistic vision of Christian education would require much greater emphasis on the reflective dimensions of Christian life.[3] Thomas Groome also stated that "good education needs to be a holistic approach to the total person – cognitive, affective, and behavioural,"[4] and more recently he emphasised that

[1] H.G. Mithra, *Wesley's Philosophy of Education for Socio-Spiritual Change* (New Delhi: Christian World Imprints, 2016), 2.

[2] Aaron J. Ghiloni, "Holistic Christian Education," ed. George Thomas Kurian and Mark A. Lamport, *Encyclopedia of Christian Education* (Maryland: Rowman & Littlefield, 2015), 595.

[3] Darcy Berube, *Religious Education at a Crossroads: Moving on in the Freedom of the Spirit* (New Jersey: Paulist Press, 1995), 56–60.

[4] Thomas Groome, *Christian Religious Education: Sharing Our Story and Vision* (San Francisco: Harper & Row, 1980), 23.

"spiritual beings need a pedagogy that engages and delves into their very souls into the depths of the human spirit."[5]

The researcher understands that Christian education is itself holistic in nature, many have restricted it only to the spiritual/ faith formation. According to H.G. Mithra, Christian education many perceive it as taught only in Christian community for faith formation, but it is with larger vision of humanity rather than narrow interest of a church, it teaches the learner to interact with both God and environment resulting in transformation of a person and society in wider sense.[6] Christian education programs must strive to inculcate in the life of learners the value of love, honesty, and care for others, equality, harmonious living in religious pluralistic context like India, and to develop right attitude of human dignity.[7] Based on these considerations mentioned above, title of this thesis reflects and emphasises the importance of holistic (spiritual, socio-cultural, intellectual, psychological and moral) transformation of the congregations through Christian education which is fundamentally holistic.

Thus in this chapter, the researcher aims to introduce the issue of holistic Christian education[8] toward transformation of the congregations and also this chapter presents the problem and elaborates the same. Further, the objectives of the study are outlined, the scope and limitations, the purpose of the study, and the hypothesis will be explained. In addition to this, the method which is to be

---

[5] Thomas Groome, *Will there Be Faith? A New Vision for Educating and Growing Disciples* (New York: HarperOne, 2011), 67.

[6] Mithra, *Wesley's Philosophy of Education for Socio-Spiritual Change*, 2.

[7] Mithra, 210.

[8] The researcher intends to emphasize on the holistic approach to Christian education that leads to the holistic transformation of the congregations. Here the researcher is aware that Christian education is itself holistic in nature but the practice of Christian education by many is considered spiritual alone. Therefore, the researcher clarifies that Christian education is concerned with the holistic transformation of the individual, church, community, and society in general. Holistic (Socio-Cultural, Spiritual, Intellectual/psychological, Moral) transformation is the aim of Christian education. Thus, the mention of Holistic Christian Education in the title has to be noted, the main concern of this thesis is holistic transformation.

employed will be explained. Furthermore, in order to understand the context of the problem, the geographical, economical, socio-cultural, and religious background of the Southern Methodist Churches in Telangana and Andhra Pradesh will be explained along with a brief historical note.

This research attempts to deliberate the role of Christian education for holistic (spiritual, socio-cultural, cognitive, and moral) transformation of the members of congregations of the Southern Methodist Churches in Telangana and Andhra Pradesh (SMCI).[9]

A. Brief Survey of the Research

The title of this Study, "Holistic Christian Education toward Transformation of Congregations of the SMCI," is mainly concerned with the transformative role of holistic approach to Christian education among SMCI. The researcher would be analysing the process of total (holistic) transformation within the congregations of the denomination through Christian education. Such an exploration will be undertaken to understand the significance of the role of Christian education that might enhance the practice of it for holistic transformation in the SMCI educational context with ideal effectiveness.

Christian education is the formation of God's people, both individual and collective, for participation in God's mission of transformation of the world. For Christian education to be relevant and authentic, and contribute to bringing change and transformation in the individual, in the church and in society it needs to maintain contextual sensitivity and integrity, and remain committed to the poorest of the poor, to faith, liberation, life and community, thus holistic approach to Christian education is inevitable. In his treatment of educators and education, R. S. Feters writes,

> "human beings inhabit a personal as well as a public world; they are circumscribed by a Nature that has to be accepted as well as transformed, that should be an object of enjoyment,

[9] Southern Methodist Churches in Telangana and Andhra Pradesh will be addressed as SMCI.

of wonder and of awe as well as material to be mastered for human purposes."[10]

The purpose of education therefore concerns both personal formation and functional formation (utility) and Christian education as "education" should share these concerns in its purpose.

Accordingly, holistic approach to Christian education for transformation is a subject that has received ample of attention in both secular and religious circles. This education is geared towards producing socially, spiritually, and mentally developed persons. Learners are introduced to the sense of responsibility, ideas of right in relation to the surrounding world and are inculcated with skills necessary for life and service.[11] By doing so, education in general helps students to attain satisfactory social adjustment, develop a responsible attitude towards life, and understand the relationship of law and freedom. From a Christian education perspective, it helps students to develop their God-given abilities, revere social and cultural values, develop physical and mental disciplines, and fashion a biblical life pattern or a life of spiritual maturity. Thus, the title is formulated to look at the feasibility of Holistic Christian Education toward the transformation of the SMCI.

B. Limitations

The intended study is confined to the SMCI. The research would concentrate on the 12 churches in the denomination within the states mentioned above. At the core of the study is an intertwining interconnectedness between what will be found to be best in both faith formation or transformation and general educational practice.

---

[10] R.S. Peters, *Essays on Educators* (London: Allen and Unwin, 1981), 87.

[11] Bernard Gechiko Nyabwari, Michael T Katola, and Daniel Muindi, "Holistic Christian Education for Character Formation in Seventh-Day Adventist Church Sponsored Secondary Schools in Nyamira County, Kenya," *International Journal of Academic Research in Progressive Education and Development* 2, no. 1 (January 2013): 245.

C. Objective of the Research

Education, as defined by Noah Webster, "the Bible (Christian Education) must be considered as the great source of all the truth by which men are to be guided in government as well as in all social transactions."[12] Webster's definition is itself a demonstration of the chief aim of Christian education - a biblical worldview. Apostle Paul, in his treatise on the value and authenticity of Scripture, explains that "All Scripture is inspired by God and is useful for teaching, for correction, for reproof, for training in righteousness, so that the man of God may be adequate, equipped for every good work" (II Timothy 3: 16-17). Based on this understanding the major tenets of this study of Holistic Christian Education toward Transformation of Congregations are:

1. To actively engage students in the teaching/learning process and encourage personal and collective responsibility;
2. Identify the instinctive potential of every member for intelligent, spiritual, social, creative, systematic thinking;
3. Holistic education encourages learners to critically approach the cultural, moral and political contexts of their lives;
4. It also values spiritual knowledge (in a non-sectarian sense). Spirituality is a state of connectedness to all life, honouring diversity in unity. It is an experience of being, belonging and caring. It is sensitivity and compassion, joy and hope. It is the harmony between the inner life and the outer life. It is the sense of wonder and reverence for the mysteries of the universe and a feeling of the purposefulness of life. It is moving towards the highest aspirations of the human spirit.

D. Proposition

Christian education is a common element or tool in any congregational ministry, but the holistic Christian education seemed to be lacking in most of the congregations which is vital in bringing out the holistic transformation within the members. Here, the researcher emphasises

---

[12] Noah Webster, "Noah Webster Quotes," *Brainy Quote* (blog), September 13, 2016, http://www.brainyquote.com/quotes/quotes/n/noahwebste394286.html. Accessed September 13, 2016.

the impartation of Christian education for holistic transformation of the congregations. Thus, the need of analysing or evaluating the method of Holistic Christian Education and its impact on the complete transformation of congregations of the SMCI is inevitable.

E. Previous Research

There are numerous inquiries done on Christian education, but the researcher has not come across any previous research that has emphasized on Holistic approach to Christian education for the complete transformation of the SMCI in particular. Therefore, the researcher has taken this inquiry for research and look at the feasibility of development taking place in all dominions of the congregations in SMCI through holistic approach to Christian education.

F. Research Methodology

As this research is on the practice of Christian education which takes place among the community of learners, I consider the Practical Research as the methodology. Practical Research is a style of methodology within the Action Research according to Clive Opie.[13] Elaine Graham cites John Swinton and Harriet Mowat to give a clear understanding on the principles of Action research as it is not so much a single discipline as "an *orientation toward inquiry* [...] and indeed a [sic] *orientation of* inquiry that seeks to create a quality of engagement, of curiosity, of question-posing through gathering evidence and testing practices."[14] The practical research is problem-centered, aims to resolve real-time issues, which generates knowledge and understanding of the problems.

Practical research offers a means of providing an understanding to a problematic situation and whether this situation concerns people or procedures is immaterial.[15] Accordingly, Kemmis and

---

[13] Clive Opie, ed., *Doing Educational Research* (New Delhi: Vistaar Publications, 2004), 81.

[14] Elaine Graham, "Is Practical Theology a Form of 'Action Research'?," *International Journal of Practical Theology* 17, no. 1 (2013): 150, https://doi.org/10.1515/ijpt-2013-0010. See also John Swinton and Harriet Mowat, *Practical Theology and Qualitative Research* (London: SCM Press, 2006), 5.

[15] Opie, *Doing Educational Research*, 79.

McTaggard encapsulate this notion, and points their view of action research as "to do action research is to plan, act, observe and reflect more carefully, more systematically, and more rigorously than one usually does in everyday life."[16] As the research is concerned with the Christian educational practices in the context of the church, which needs a carefully and systematically planned, acted, observed, and reflected study. Practical research methodology is an appropriate research style that is feasible to achieve the purpose of study.

1. Literature Review

The literature review will provide theoretical authority to the development of the Structure of Transformation. A review of this literature, offering a biblical, historical, foundation for the teaching of religious education will be outlined, with a view to identifying what best practice in facilitating the goal of both holistic approach to Christian education and the consequential transformation.

Number of spiritual, academic, and sociological disciplines offers the vital ingredients on which to base some pivotal decisions with regard to developing holistic Christian education. It is done by exploring books, journals, periodicals, dictionaries, encyclopaedias, magazines, unpublished materials, local bulletins, and online materials in the process of research.

2. Empirical Study

In this research data collection technique is used for conducting survey through questionnaires with the help of sampling elements. Two sets of questionnaires were distributed in person.

A. First set of questionnaire was given to the pastors and the leaders of the SMCI who are involved in fulltime or part-time preaching or teaching ministry of the denomination. They were selected on the bases of maturity and understanding of the importance of Christian education in the church context.

[16] S. Kemmis and R. McTaggart, eds., *The Action Research Planner*, 3rd ed. (Victoria: Deakin University Press, 1992), 10.

B. The second set of questionnaire was distributed to the randomly selected members of SMCI. This includes adults, youth, women, men, teenagers, and Sunday school teachers.

This data collected is analysed to come to conclusions and make recommendations for the proposed inquiry.

3. Sampling

The researcher used the random sampling method to distribute the questionnaires to 12 churches that belong to SMCI. 20 members were selected randomly from each of these churches which includes men and women of different age groups. 22 pastors and church leaders were also selected for the same.

G. Definitions of Key Terms

1. Holistic Christian Education

Contemporary religious education is better able to contribute to human wholeness, health, and freedom when its pedagogical praxis is shaped from the holistic perspective. Kate Siejk understands the holistic perspective as a way of looking at everything that result from a new way of thinking. It is a perspective Christian educators acquire when they recognize the malignant effects of the contradictious thinking that is not inherent to, but has been built into, all levels of religious education.[17] Holistic, a concept noted in the thesis title refers to the intentional attempt to overcome the rational/emotional contradiction identified as a traditional and contemporary challenge, and fuse together both realms so that faith formation can be more complete, balanced, and authentic.[18]

---

[17] Kate Siejk, "Toward a Holistic Religious Education: Reflections and Pedagogical Possibilities," in *Association of Professors and Researchers in Religious Education Conference* (Fort Worth, Texas: Gonzaga University, 1993), 271.

[18] Siejk, 272.

2. Holistic Education[19]

Holistic education, in contrast to progressive education, sees the child as an emerging spiritual being within a larger planetary and cosmic ecology that extends beyond social and political realities. In holistic education one must respond to the learner with an open, inquisitive mind and a loving heart, and a sensitive understanding of the world he or she is growing into.[20] This definition is appropriately articulated, which can be taken in a broader sense for the research.

3. Christian Education

According to Campbell Wyckoff, Christian education is defined as,

> "the guided process of helping growing persons to achieve at each stage of their growth such habits, skills, attitudes, appreciation, knowledge, ideas, ideals, and intentions as will enable them at each stage to achieve an ever more integrated personality, competent and satisfying living in their social environment, and increasing co-operatives with God and man in the reconstruction of the society into a fellowship of persons."[21]

For Akheto Sema, Christian religious education is a process in which teaching-learning takes place concerning Christian faith and beliefs in the lives of an individual, family, and the church as a whole.[22]

4. Transformation

The following is the definition of transformation, which was given by a group of Christian leaders and theologians following

---

[19] Holistic education reflects and responds more fully than conventional education to a new and increasingly accepted view of what it means to be human as well as to much popular social criticism.

[20] Ron Miller, *What Are Schools For? Holistic Education in American Culture*, 3rd Edition (Brandon, VT: Holistic Education Press, 1997), 5.

[21] Campbell D. Wyckoff, *The Task of Christian Education* (Philadelphia: The Westminster Press, n.d.), 18.

[22] Akheto Sema, *Understanding the Nature and Purpose of Christian Religious Education* (Delhi: ISPCK, 2011), 1.

a 1996 consultative conference in Chicago as quoted by Noel Roxas, it reads: "Transformation is the change from a condition of human existence contrary to God's purposes to one in which people are able to enjoy fullness of life in harmony with God."[23] According to Merriam Webster Online Dictionary, transformation is, the act or process of changing completely: a complete change or a complete or major change in someone's or something's appearance, form, etc.[24]

5. Holistic Transformation

Bryant Myers use the term transformational development to reflect his concern for seeking positive change in the whole of human life materially, socially and spiritually that is holistic. Changed people and just and peaceful relationships are the twin goals of transformation, those who have discovered their true identity as children of God and who have recovered their true vocation as faithful and productive stewards of gifts from God for the well-being of all.[25]

6. Congregation

Merriam Webster Online Dictionary defines congregation as, an assembly of persons: gathering; *especially*: an assembly of persons met for worship and religious instruction: a religious community: an organized body of believers in a particular locality.[26]

H. Background of Telangana and Andhra Pradesh

1. Historical Background

Telugu speaking people in Indian epic literature first appears at the time of the death of the Mauryan Emperor Ashoka in 232 BC, this date has been considered to be the beginning of the Andhra

[23] Noel S. Roxas, "Transformation" (November 8, 2014), 2.

[24] "Transformation," *Merriam Webster Online Dictionary*, http://www.merriam-webster.com/dictionary/transformation. Accessed September 16, 2015.

[25] Bryant Myers, *Walking with the Poor: Principles and Practices of Transformational Development* (Maryknoll: Orbis Books, 1998), 3, 14.

[26] "Congregations," *Merriam Webster Online Dictionary*, http://www.merriam-webster.com/dictionary/congregations. Accessed September 16, 2015.

historical record. Various dynasties have ruled the area, including the Satavahana dynasty, Sakas, Andhra Ikshvakus, Eastern Chalukyas, Pallava dynasty, Pandyan dynasty, Chola dynasty, Telugu Cholas, the Bobbili, the Vijayanagara Empire, the Qutub Shahi dynasty of Golconda, the Nizams of Hyderabad and the Kakatiya dynasty.[27] The first great Andhra empire was that of the Satavahanas, who came to power when the last Kanva emperor Sisuman, was assassinated by his Prime Minister Sipraca, of the Andhra tribe. They reigned for 450 years and the last was Puliman or Puloma the pious, who later on put an end to his life by drowning himself in the holy waters of the Ganges River, after the example of his grandfather.[28] While in the west the inhabitants of the Gangetic provinces were denominated Andhra Hindus. The Satavahana rulers are said to have been held in the highest veneration all over India; and their fame was extended to the Malay Archipelago, the Maharajas of India being a favourite subject of Malayan poetry.[29]

2. Geographical Background

Located on the uplands of Deccan plateau, Telangana is the link between the North and South of India. It is thus no surprise that the region on the whole came to be known for its Ganga-Jamuna *Tehzeeb*[30] and the capital Hyderabad as a 'miniature India.'

Andhra Pradesh was formed on 1st November, 1956 under the States' reorganization scheme. It was the fifth largest State with an area of 2,76,754 sq. km, accounting for 8.4% of India's territory before the bifurcation of it into two states in 2014. The State has the

---

[27] R Srihari, "Sanskrit and Telugu Literature," in *Proceedings of the Andhra Pradesh Oriental Conference: Fourth Session, Nagarjuna University, Guntur, 3rd to 5th March 1984* (Andhra Pradesh Oriental Conference, Michigan: University of Michigan, 1984), 105.

[28] Thomas Burrow, *Collected Papers on Dravidian Linguistics* (Madras: Annamalai University, 1968), 18.

[29] Josiah Conder, *The Modern Traveller: A Popular Description, Geographical, Historical, and Topographical of the Various Countries of the Globe*, vol. 1 (London: James Duncan, 1828), 141.

[30] Muslim Meaning: The name Tahzeeb is a Muslim baby name, which means Culture.

longest coastline (972 km) among all the States in India.[31] Telangana is a newly constituted state from Andhra Pradesh in Southern region of India. A major quantity of Telangana was part of princely state of Hyderabad (Medak and Warangal Divisions), when it was ruled by Nizams under British rule till 1947 and later until 1948. In 1956, Andhra Pradesh was merged with Telangana region after dissolution of Hyderabad state and Andhra Pradesh was formed. However, Telangana became the 29th state of India on June 2, 2014.[32] The capital of Telangana state is Hyderabad and it comprises of 10 districts and Andhra Pradesh has 13 districts. As per the India States' Reorganization Act recommendations a resolution was passed in the Lok Sabha and Rajya Sabha which was gazetted by the President of India which led to the bifurcation of the state, and Hyderabad will serve as the joint capital of Andhra Pradesh and Telangana for the next 10 years that is till 2024.[33] Bordering states of Telangana & Andhra Pradesh include Odisha and Chhattisgarh to the north, Maharashtra, Karnataka to the west and Tamilnadu in the south, and Bay of Bengal Sea to the East.

Southern Methodist Churches were established in the state of Andhra Pradesh from 2007 and the state was bifurcated later in 2014. Therefore, the presence of this new denomination in these two new states of Telangana and Andhra Pradesh. Thus, the mention of these two states in the title of the research, and researcher proposes to identify these two states as one state for the purpose of this research as Southern Methodist Churches were planted in the two states.

---

[31] Jakob Basista, "India," ed. George Thomas Kurian, *Encyclopaedia of the World's Nations and Cultures* (New Delhi: Viva Books, 2007), 1081.

[32] "Profile of Telangana," *Telangana Online* (blog), September 14, 2016, http://www.telanganaonline.in/About/Profile/index.html. Accessed September 14, 2016.

[33] "Andhra Pradesh State Profile," PDF, *National Institute of Disaster Management*, http://nidm.gov.in/PDF/DP/ANDHRA.pdf. Accessed September 14, 2016.

3. Socio-Cultural Background

The Telugu people are a Dravidian[34] ethno-linguistic group. The majority of Telugus reside in the states of Andhra Pradesh and Telangana. The Telugu language is the most-spoken Dravidian language, the third-most spoken language in India[35] and the fourth most in the Indian subcontinent, following Hindi, Bengali and Punjabi. Culturally and socially, Andhra Pradesh and Telangana have many similarities with the other South Indian states like, Tamilnadu, Karnataka, and Kerala. South Indian culture though with its visible differences forms an important part of the Indian culture, it is essentially the celebration of the eternal universe through the celebration of the beauty of the body and motherhood.[36] It is exemplified through its dance,[37] clothing,[38] and sculptures. Telangana and Andhra Pradesh are 'South of North and North of South,' which have long been a meeting place for diverse languages and cultures.[39]

4. Economical Background

The Economy of Telangana is mainly driven by agriculture. Two important rivers of India, the Godavari and Krishna, flow through

---

[34] Dravidians are native speakers of any of the Dravidian languages of South India. There are around 220 million native speakers of Dravidian languages. They form the majority of the population of South India. Dravidian-speaking people are natively found in India, Pakistan, Afghanistan, Nepal, Maldives, Bangladesh, and Sri Lanka. See Barbara A. West, "Dravidian," *Encyclopaedia of the Peoples of Asia and Oceania* (New York: Infobase Publishers, 2010), 194.

[35] Bharti Jain, "Nearly 60% of Indians Speak a Language Other than Hindi," *The Times of India*, June 21, 2014, Delhi edition, http://timesofindia.indiatimes.com/india/Nearly-60-of-Indians-speak-a-language-other-than-Hindi/articleshow/36922157.cms. Accessed September 14 2016.

[36] Brenda Beck, "The Symbolic Merger of Body, Space, and Cosmos in Hindu Tamil Nadu," *Contributions to Indian Sociology* 10, no. 2 (1976): 218.

[37] Bharata, *The Natyashastra*, trans. Manmohan Ghosh (Calcutta: Manisha Granthalaya, 1967), 14.

[38] Susan Wadley, *The Powers of Tamil Women* (Syracuse: Syracuse University Press, 1980), 3.

[39] "Language and Culture," *Telangana State Portal Official* (blog), September 16, 2016, http://www.telangana.gov.in/About/Language. Accessed September 16, 2016.

the state, providing irrigation. Farmers in Telangana mainly depend on rain-fed water sources for irrigation. Rice is the major food crop. Other important crops are cotton, sugar cane, mango and tobacco. Recently, crops used for vegetable oil production such as sunflower and peanuts have gained favour. There are many multi-state irrigation projects in development, including Godavari River Basin Irrigation Projects and Nagarjuna Sagar Dam, the world's highest masonry dam.[40]

The state has also started to focus on the fields of information technology and biotechnology. Telangana is one of top IT (Information Technology) exporting states of India. There are 68 Special Economic Zones in the state.[41] Telangana also is a mineral-rich state, with coal reserves at Singareni Collieries Company.

Andhra Pradesh was ranked eighth among other Indian states in terms of Gross State Domestic Product[42] for the financial year 2014–15. The GSDP at current prices was ₹5200.3 billion and at constant prices was ₹2645.21 billion. The domestic product of agriculture sector give rise to ₹545.99 billion (US$8.1 billion) and Industrial sector for ₹507.45 billion (US$7.5 billion). The service sector of the state accounts more percentage of the GSDP with a total of ₹1,305.87 billion (US$19 billion).[43] In the 2010 list by *Forbes* magazine, there were several from Andhra Pradesh among the top 100 richest Indians.[44]

---

[40] "Economic Development of Telangana," *Agricultural Department of Telangana*, http://agri.ap.nic.in/. Accessed September 16, 2016.

[41] Adopted from, "Special Economic Zones of Andhra Pradesh," PDF, *SEZ India*, https://web.archive.org/web/20091007035200/http://www.sezindia.nic.in/HTMLS/578FormalapprovalsgrantedunderSEZAct19thJune,09.pdf. Accessed September 16, 2016.

[42] Gross State Domestic Product (GSDP) is defined as a measure, in monetary terms, of the volume of all goods and services produced within the boundaries of the State during a given period of time, accounted without duplication.

[43] "Economy of Andhra Pradesh," PDF, *Andhra Pradesh State Portal Official*, http://www.ap.gov.in/AP%20State%20Statistical%20Abstract%20May%202014/4_AP_Economy.pdf. Accessed September 16, 2016.

[44] "India's Richest," *Forbes.com*, http://www.forbes.com/lists/2010/77/india-rich-10_Indias-Richest_Rank.html. Accessed September 16, 2016.

5. Religious Background

People of Andhra Pradesh and Telangana are highly pious, who follow their religion with the highest regard. In these two states, the major religions are Hinduism, Islam, Christianity and Buddhism. Around the states, you can find people following different religious practices, along with their own notions and customs. Numerous temples, mosques, churches and stupas thrive in the length and breadth of the state. However, Hinduism is the major religion that is followed by maximum number of people. Muslims are by and large concentrated in Hyderabad and Secunderabad cities that stand second, and Christianity, Buddhism, Jainism follows the list. The tribal people have their own religion and worship nature.

According to the 2011 census, the Andhra Pradesh state's population, (before the state's bifurcation, hence includes religious affiliation from neighbouring Telangana too) this does not reflect the current religious affiliation in Andhra Pradesh formed as of 2 July 2014, religious data for Andhra Pradesh is around 91.25% Hindu with a Muslim minority of 6.25% along with smaller numbers of Christians, Jains, Sikhs, and Buddhists.[45]

I. Christianity in Telangana and Andhra Pradesh

Telugu Christians or Telugu Kraistava[46] are an ethno-religious community who form the second-largest religious minority in the Indian states of Andhra Pradesh and Telangana. According to the Census of India, there are over a million Christians in Andhra Pradesh constituting 1.5% of the state's population, although a decrease from the 1971 census figure which was 4.2%, as a result of low birth rates and emigration.[47]

---

[45] "Population by Religious Community," 2011 CENSUS, *Government of India: Ministry of Home Affairs*, http://www.censusindia.gov.in/2011census/C-01.html. Accessed September 19, 2016.

[46] A Telugu term used for Christians.

[47] "Population by Religious Community."

1. Denominations

Most Telugu Christians are Protestant belonging to major Indian Protestant denominations such as the predominant Anglican Church of South India, the Andhra Evangelical Lutheran Church, Methodist Church in India, Samavesam of Telugu Baptist Churches, Bible Mission, the Salvation Army, and several others. There also is a significant number of Roman Catholics, Independent Evangelicals and Pentecostals.

2. History

Although the Franciscans of the Roman Catholic Church brought Christianity to the Deccan area in 1535, it is only after 1759 AD, when the Northern Circars came under the rule of the East India Company, that the region opened up to greater Christian influence. The first Protestant missionaries in Andhra Pradesh were Rev. Cran and Rev. Des Granges who were sent out by the London Missionary Society. They set up their station at Visakhapatnam in 1805 AD.[48]

3. Location

Regions with significant populations of Telugu Christians include the erstwhile Northern Circars, the coastal belt and the cities of Hyderabad and Secunderabad. Many Telugu Christians have immigrated to other countries in the Anglo sphere with significant populations being present in the United States, United Kingdom and Australia.[49]

4. In Society

The Christian Church in Andhra Pradesh and Telangana runs thousands of educational institutions and hospitals contributing significantly to the development of the state. Telugu Christians are found in all walks of life and have contributed much to the development of the state. Telugu Christians have one of the highest

[48] Sherring Smith, *History of Christianity in India* (Madras: Christian Literature Society, 1895), 127–30.

[49] Joshua Pilli, "UECF History," *United Evangelical Christian Fellowship*, http://www.uecf.net/history.htm. Accessed November 1, 2016.

literacy, work participation figures and most even male-to-female ratio figures among the various religious communities in the state.[50]

J. Brief History of Southern Methodist Church in India

Methodism was introduced in America by George Whitefield, Robert Strawbridge, Philip Embury and others, the former having come to America prior to 1744. The first conference of Methodist church was held in 1773. The Methodism developed leaps and bounds in the United States after its first General Conference in 1845 under the name of Methodist Episcopal Church, South until 1938.[51] The Birmingham General Conference of The Methodist Episcopal Church, South met in Louisville, Kentucky, on May 1, 1938 decided to enter into a union with the Methodist Episcopal Church and the Methodist Protestant Church. This union was opposed by layman's organization of the Methodist Episcopal Church, South, who later on formed another church to preserve the Holiness movement proposed by the founder of Methodism, John Wesley who had their first Annual Session in 1940 at Turbeville, South Carolina. This development led to the official formation of the Southern Methodist Church which has four Annual Conferences at present with a membership of more than 100 churches in the United States.[52] The Southern Methodist Church had been working in various countries, which also extended their mission work to India.

Southern Methodist Church in India (SMCI) is an evangelical bible believing denomination which started establishing churches in Andhra Pradesh and Telangana since 2007. SMCI started its work with Word India an approved mission organization of the Southern Methodist Church (SMC), an independent evangelical Methodist denomination headquartered in Orangeburg, South Carolina, USA. Word India officially merged with SMC, USA. Word India was

[50] Bal Patil, "NATIONAL MINORITY STATUS FOR JAIN COMMUNITY IN INDIA," *The India Post*, July 11, 2008, sec. Religion, http://www.theindiapost.com/articles/national-minority-status-for-jain-community-in-india/. Accessed November 1, 2016.

[51] "History of Southern Methodist Church," *The Southern Methodist Church, Official Website*, http://www.thesmc.org/aboutus.html. Accessed October 31, 2016.

[52] "History of Southern Methodist Church."

headed by Rev. Moses Boosa a former pastor with Methodist Church in India (MCI), Hyderabad, India.[53] Being a strong Wesleyan he joined SMC under the leadership of Rev. Bedford Landers the former President of SMC, USA and Rev. Dr. John T. Hucks Jr the present President. Rev. Moses' credentials were officially transferred to SMC in the year 2007. The Eastern Annual Conference of SMC, USA received Rev. Moses into full connection after 2 years.[54] Since 2007, the denomination is establishing its work in the state of Andhra Pradesh (later it was bifurcated into two states as Telangana and Andhra Pradesh) and it has already planted 12 churches.

Conclusion

An overview of the problem of holistic Christian education imparted in the churches, and the methods which the researcher intends to carry out throughout the research has been introduced in the chapter. The geographical background and the brief history of SMCI provide understanding of the intended research. The statement, objectives, purpose, elaboration of the problem and the hypothesis are equally directed towards holistic transformation of the congregations and for the future of the SMCI. The following chapter will review and evaluate the holistic Christian education toward complete transformation of the congregations based on the previous literature.

---

[53] Dale Linder Altman, "SMC President Visits Churches in India," *The Times and Democrat*, September 15, 2013, http://thetandd.com/lifestyles/magazine/smc-president-visits-churches-in-india/article_9de49248-1cdd-11e3-b280-0019bb2963f4.html. Accessed September 28, 2016.

[54] "About Us," *Southern Methodist Church in India*, http://www.southernmethodistchurch.in/. Accessed September 28, 2016.

Chapter 2

Conceptual Framework of Holistic Christian Education and Transformation

Introduction

This chapter presents a review of literature with an intention to create an understanding for the study of holistic Christian education towards (total) transformation of the congregations with special reference to SMCI. The Biblical understanding of religious education is the foundation established for the Jewish education in Old Testament and Christian education in the New Testament. This reinforces the basic evaluation of the role of Christian education in the holistic transformation since the inception of the church in the early centuries and the middle Ages. The researcher points out the meaning, concept, and purpose of (holistic) Christian education by various authors and brings out the glimpses about the understanding of the transformation. At the later stage of the chapter, the researcher has brought out the vital aspects of the research study, role of Christian education in the holistic transformation (spiritual, socio-cultural, intellectual or psychological, and moral transformation), and a brief enlightenment on how the church has to involve in the holistic transformational ministry.

A. Biblical Understanding of Religious Education

In order to understand that holistic transformation of the congregations through Christian education is practical, one should have the basic understanding of the origins, of Christian education. The aims of Christian education depends upon the conception of the religion on the one hand, and upon the conception of education on the other.[55] From the earliest times, the Hebrews considered education and training of the common people as of supreme importance. The spirit of their education was intensely religious; the distinction between "sacred" and "secular" which has proved a serious detriment to education in modern times, did not exist.[56] "The fear of Jehovah is the beginning of knowledge," says a wise man (Proverbs 1:7), to which a later sage adds that it is also its "fullness and crown" (Ecclesiastes 1:16, 18). This understanding leads to the holistic nature of the religious education in the Bible.

Old Testament scholarship has long recognized a double origin for Israel's educational origins: the first, beginning with the call of Abraham and the second, with Moses and the Exodus.[57] The Israelites were called to understand themselves as the people of God and to come to know how they may serve the Lord who had called them. The primary aim of the entire educational activity was religious (Genesis 18:19), and was to train the young to know and serve the Lord (Deuteronomy 6:7; Proverbs 1:7) apart from being trained into moral, social, and cultural beings, so that throughout their life they would not depart from this way (Proverbs 22:6). Thus, religious education centred its attention on the Torah and aimed at educating the Jews for everyday living.

---

[55] B.S. Winchester, "Religious Education, Aims of," ed. John T. McFarland et al., *The Encyclopaedia of Sunday Schools and Religious Education* (New York: Thomas Nelson & Sons, 1915), 890.

[56] F.C Eiselen, "Education in Old Testament Times," ed. John T. McFarland and Benjamin S. Winchester, *The Encyclopaedia of Sunday Schools and Religious Education* (New York: Thomas Nelson & Sons, 1915), 363.

[57] I Aron et al., "Jewish Education," ed. Iris V. Cully and Kendig Brubaker Cully, *Harper's Encyclopedia of Religious Education* (New York: Harper & Row, 1990), 334.

B. Jewish Education in the Old Testament Times

Right from the book of Genesis to the book of Malachi in the Old Testament there are various individuals involved in educating the people of Israel. Old Testament Jewish Education can also be separated into three divisions: 1. From Moses to Josiah (c. 1200 B.C.), 2. From the reform of Josiah to Ezra (c. 621 B.C.), and 3. From arrival of Ezra to Jerusalem to the Maccabean Age (c. 458 B.C. to c. 160 B.C.).[58] Most of these educators of Old Testament were correcting and instructing people in spirituality, social relationships, cultural identity, moral development, and psychological transformation.

1. Jewish Education's link with Religion

Three events stand out in the history of Jewish education. They centre on three persons, Ezra, Simon ben-Shetah, and Joshua ben-Gamala.[59] It was Ezra who established Scripture as the basis for schooling, and his successors went on to make the synagogue a place of instruction as well as a place of worship.[60] Simon ben-Shetah enacted, in about 75 B.C., that elementary schooling should be compulsory. Joshua ben-Gamala improved existing organization, appointing teachers in every province and town, a century later.[61] By this it can be observed that the worship place was also a place of instruction, where people of all age groups were instructed.

Traditionally, Jewish education began in the home when a child was about three years old and continued throughout childhood and adult life. Similarly, the church today has to give importance of education not only limited to the children in the church, but also to all age groups. The study of Torah was a commandment incumbent upon all Jews and was seen as the foundation for the other commandments. Formal schooling usually began at the age of six and was conducted in schools associated to synagogues that

---

[58] Eiselen, "Education in Old Testament Times," 364.

[59] Eiselen, 364.

[60] D.F. Payne, "Education," ed. J.D. Douglas, *The New Bible Dictionary* (Grand Rapids: WM B. Eerdmans, 1979), 336.

[61] Payne, 336.

belonged to Judaism, the religion of Jews.[62] Ezra made more definite the linking of religion with education in everyday life.[63] Therefore, the Jewish education was intertwined with the religious beliefs of the Jews and to the everyday socio-cultural life, which appears to be holistic in nature.

2. Personnel involved in Jewish Education

Instruction in the traditional and accepted ways or heritage provides continuity across the generations, especially in times of transition and change.[64] Walter Brueggemann identifies this component "instruction" in the Old Testament Canon as the *ethos* of the Torah, the disclosure of that which is binding upon faith community.[65] A faith community needs leaders to be instructed and it should find some way to generate them, choose them, appoint them, and assign specific functions for them to perform. In ancient Israel, one hear about three distinct types of religious leaders in the role of instruction – priest, prophet, and wisdom teacher.[66] By looking at each of these in some detail, perhaps we can learn something about the religious educational needs for the contemporary church.

a. Priests

The history of the formal priesthood in Israel begins with the time of the Exodus. In the patriarchal times the heads of families offered sacrifices and intercessory prayers, and performed general religious functions, instructing the people, but there seems to have been no specialization and no separate priestly office, as there was among the Egyptians (Genesis 47:22, 26).[67] The blessing of Levi by Moses

---

[62] Aron et al., "Jewish Education," 335.

[63] Payne, "Education," 336.

[64] Robert W. Pazmino, *Foundational Issues in Christian Education*, Second Edition (Grand Rapids: Baker Books, 1997), 18.

[65] Walter Brueggemann, *Creative Word: Canon as a Model for Biblical Education* (Minneapolis: Fortress Press, 1982), 108.

[66] Daniel J. Simundson, "Priest, Prophet, Wisdom Teacher: Old Testament Models of the Minister," *Word & World* IX, no. 4 (Fall 1989): 351.

[67] James Oliver Buswell Jr, "Priest, Priesthood," ed. Merrill C. Tenney and Steven Barabas, *The Zondervan Pictorial Bible Dictionary* (Grand Rapids: Zondervan,

(Deuteronomy 33:10) gives an indication of what the priest was called to do: "They shall teach Jacob thy ordinances and Israel thy law; they shall put incense before thee, and whole burnt offering upon thy altar." Teach the Torah and tend to the altar – it sounds like 'Spiritual' and 'Secular' ministry which appeals to the socio-cultural, spiritual, cognitive, moral aspect of the people's life.

b. Prophets

In continuation of the role of priest in the educational life of the Jews, some prophets were also involved as priests - e.g., Jeremiah, Ezekiel, maybe Isaiah. So, these functions are not necessarily mutually exclusive. The prophet, unlike the priest, was less likely to appeal to past tradition but did something similar by warning the people and instructing them to consider the Law of God as vital for all aspects of life.[68] The prophet was more likely to appeal to special revelation, a divine appointment.[69] Because of his special appointment, the prophet was free to challenge and severely criticize existing religious, social and political institutions. Post-exilic prophets did speak words of comfort, Ezekiel ministered to exiles in Babylon.[70] But, in spite of these examples, the primary task of the prophet was not just to tend to the spiritual care of the flock but to address the issues that are related to other aspects in the society.

c. Wisdom Teachers

The role of the teacher of wisdom tends to be less emphasized in our thinking than the ministry functions of the priest and prophet. Perhaps this has something to do with the anti-intellectualism in both church and society. God is the great teacher of the Bible, Jesus being the supreme expression of this divine teacher, showing compassion combined with clarity, power and authority in His instruction had

---

1963), 682.

[68] Simundson, "Priest, Prophet, Wisdom Teacher: Old Testament Models of the Minister," 353.

[69] David W. Bercot, ed., "Prophecy, Prophets," *A Dictionary of Early Christian Beliefs* (Massachusetts: Hendrickson Publishers, 1998), 540.

[70] Simundson, "Priest, Prophet, Wisdom Teacher: Old Testament Models of the Minister," 354.

great influence in the total life of ancient Israel.[71] The whole course of Biblical story can be viewed as God's instruction. God can be found instructing with commandments and object lessons in Eden,[72] and the giving of the law at Mount Sinai is for Israel an exemplary teaching event. His aim was to transform the humans into holistic beings.

C. Christian Education in New Testament

It is to be noted that Christianity, as we know it today from the New Testament, has been greatly influenced by Judaism (Jewish education). To this end Charles Benton Eavey argued, "Jesus and the apostles reverenced the teachings of the Old Testament though they spoke out forcefully against the ideas and opinions of men that had corrupted God's revelation."[73] Therefore in many ways, Christianity was modelled after Judaism. This should come as no surprise for Christianity originates from Judaism.

In the New Testament, as in the Old Testament, teaching begins with God; in this case with Jesus Christ Himself, hence Christian education. The Holy Spirit is also referred to as the teacher, enabling believers to teach and giving gifts of teaching to the church. Further, Jesus commanded His followers to teach, which they did. Thus in short, in the New Testament, in one way or another, every Christian is a teacher. What stands out glaringly is that Christian education constituted a very important component of the entire ministry that includes the holistic transformation of the New Testament church.

1. Jesus, the Teacher

Jesus was the Teacher. He was the first person to teach in a New Testament sense. Nicodemus referred to Him as a teacher come from God (John 3:2). More than anything else the Gospels portray Jesus as a teacher. Forty five times He is referred to as a teacher and fourteen times as a Rabbi. He was a teacher par excellence. Eavey emphasized

---

[71] Leland Ryken, James C. Wilhoit, and Tremper Longman III, eds., "Teacher, Teaching," *Dictionary of Biblical Imagery* (Downers Grove: InterVarsity Press, 1998), 842.

[72] Ryken, Wilhoit, and Longman III, 842.

[73] C.B. Eavey, *History of Christian Education* (Chicago: Moody Press, 1964), 76.

this attributing to Jesus, "He used teaching as a chief means of accomplishing what He had come into the world to do. That was to show men the way to God and to shape their attitudes, ideals and conduct to conform to God's will. Teaching was His business. He was often a healer, sometimes a worker of miracles, frequently a preacher, but always a teacher."[74] Attitudes, ideals, and conduct is the concern of Jesus which is to be transformed toward the will of God, thus, it shows that His teaching ministry was mainly holistic. He can be termed as the best Holistic Teacher in the history of mankind.

It is useful to picture Jesus in at least three seasons of life when it comes to his total human development and maturation:[75] 1) Infancy – when he was nurtured spiritually at home, Luke 2:1-40, 2) Childhood – up to the age of twelve years – summarizes the disciplined life of Jesus, Luke 2: 41-52, and 3) Middle adulthood (last three years of his life) – except confession and sinfulness, Jesus experienced all the disciplines of a normal person, like adult maturation.

2. Apostles and Disciples as Teachers

The whole of the New Testament abounds with teaching experiences and lessons. It is important to note that the writings in the New Testament are teachings in themselves. They arose out of varying circumstances; were intended to address specific situations, however, in the final analysis, they are teaching lessons themselves. In this case, the words of Paul to Timothy about the writings of the Old Testament hold true also for the New Testament writings. "All Scripture is inspired by God and is useful for teaching the truth, rebuking error, correcting faults, and giving instruction for right living ..." (II Timothy 3:16).

From the coming of the Holy Spirit and the resultant conversion of many Jews, teaching of apostolic doctrine went on daily (Acts 2:42). Peter taught on the day of Pentecost in his famous sermon (Acts 2: 13-40). Preaching was teaching. Whereas there was in the early church,

---

[74] Eavey, 78.

[75] Ronald T. Habermas, *Introduction to Christian Education and Formation: A Lifelong Plan for Christ-Centered Restoration* (Grand Rapids: Zondervan, 2008), 62–63.

much preaching, fellowship, healing and miracles, teaching seemed to have dominated the ministry of apostles. Teaching and preaching went together, "And every day in the temple and in people's homes they continued to teach and preach the good news ..." (Acts 5:42). This good news could be termed as the gospel which the researcher looks into it as the 'holistic gospel'. Jim Harries critiqued the holistic gospel stating that it has arisen from a combination of linguistic misunderstandings, guilt, and jealousy from the great economic disparities that exist in today's world.[76] But, holistic here means all the aspects of humanity is transformed through the teaching and preaching of the good news; good news appealed to every aspect of life not just spirituality, since the beginning of the church in the early centuries to this day.

3. Holy Spirit, the Teacher

In the Old Testament God was portrayed as a Teacher. Jesus Christ was also a Teacher par excellence in the New Testament. The Holy Spirit, the third person in the trinity, is also a Teacher. All in all, God in His three Persons is a Teacher.[77] The Holy Spirit is portrayed as a Teacher, first, because Jesus said about Him that when He comes He will teach the disciples everything and make them remember all that which He had told them (John 14:26). As a Teacher, Holy Spirit guides people into all truth (John 16:13), and to teachers, He gives gifts of teaching, knowledge and discernment (I Cor. 12:8-11; Eph. 4:11). Second, The Holy Spirit would illuminate the understanding of the disciples. Third, the Holy Spirit reveals truth about God so that that which was not known is revealed and known (John 15:26). In the fourth instance, the Holy Spirit is a Teacher because He transforms both teacher and student alike. Finally, the Spirit facilitates the work of Christian education.[78] The ministry of the Holy Spirit appeals to the total personality of an individual, thus

[76] Jim Harries, "Critiquing the Holistic Gospel," *Alliance for Vulnerable Mission Bulletin*, April 2013, 1.

[77] Eavey, *History of Christian Education*, 82.

[78] "The Holy Spirit as Teacher," *Knowing Jesus*, http://bible.knowing-jesus.com/topics/The-Holy-Spirit-As-Teacher. Accessed November 11, 2016.

His work is aimed at the holistic transformation of the individual, church, community, and society in general.

D. History of Christian Education

Christian Education in Early Church has its beginning in the teaching of Jesus. Jesus taught perfectly in His time with full authority, and everything He taught, He testified with His life. To accomplish His task He used the model of teaching as the most important tool. Jesus meant to show the way of God and "to shape their attitude, ideals, and conduct to conform the God's will."[79] The complete person is the first and foremost priority in His ministry. He gave the commission of continuing task to reach the whole nation.

1. Christian Education in Apostolic Period

After the ascension of Jesus, the day of Pentecost was the first response to the great commission of Jesus.[80] Later the teaching occurred in two places- the Christian meeting and the Christian home. The Christian meeting has 3 kinds -[81] firstly; they get together which meant for the teaching of scripture for the purpose of edification. Secondly, this meeting meant to have common meal or love feast, which was followed by the Lord's Supper which signifies the fellowship and concern for one another. Thirdly, the Christian meeting took place when the Christian community had business to transact Church discipline, which was not incidental to the strength and purity of the fellowship. This is to be understood that the development of social relationships took place in the early church. The later place, i.e., the Christian family was the most prominent place to acquire Christian knowledge. The teaching of Old Testament had great influence that family is the primary source of Christian Education.[82] The Hellenistic nature and its political ideology of Roman culture shaped the development of Early Christian Education. Educating

---

[79] Eavey, *History of Christian Education*, 78.

[80] Eavey, 29.

[81] Kenneth O. Gangel and Warren S. Benson, *Christian Education: Its History and Philosophy* (Chicago: Moody Press, 1983), 79.

[82] Gangel and Benson, 79.

children was of twofold-[83] 1) they provide instruction which could help children to grasp Christian Doctrine, 2) and to strengthen them with Christian values and live practically within the secular culture covered in the rhetorical and philosophical studies of the pagan schools.

2. Christian Education in the Epistles

With the effect of the Pentecost, all the members become learners for they must learn everything that the Lord commanded; and they must obey what they had learned. The Epistles of Acts, Hebrew and Ephesians is the record how Church implemented Christ's command.[84] The Church of Antioch had to provide different levels of instruction as they were integrated with the gentile community, their educational strategy demanded some creative methods which were focussed on education. Barnabas became the first educational consultant on a remedial education programme. Later the Church of Antioch was large enough and by which they adopted an educational strategy to accommodate the unprecedented developments in Antioch.[85] Hebrew 5: 11-14, the unnamed author rebukes everyone because they were slow learners and ought to have been teachers. The author in 5:12 implies 'milk' as the basic food for beginners and 'solid food' meant to the believers those needed to build on the practise what they already knew. Ephesians 4:7-16 implies of the purpose and special abilities of the believers which works doesn't meant isolated act however it is to achieve the larger objectives with complex coordination efforts. In line with this Paul asserts the body of Christ functions best when everyone contributes (I Corinth 12:7).[86]

[83] Gangel and Benson, 81.

[84] Michael S. Lawson and Rober J. Choun, *Directing Christian Education: The Changing Role of Christian Education Specialist* (Chicago: Moody Press, 1992), 17.

[85] Lawson and Choun, 17–18.

[86] Lawson and Choun, 19–20.

3. Formal Schools in Early Church

Christianity has its historical roots so deeply embedded in Hebrew history and traditions.[87] During the early church period the church took the responsibility of instructing all the basic knowledge to all members within the faith community. The church founded certain schools fot the believers.

a. Catechumenal Schools

Catechumenal Schools were established in the first and second centuries and were designed to train converts, both young and old for church membership. The "*catechumens*" were children of believers, adult Jews, and gentile converts. The "*catechumen*" and "*catechism*" are derived from Greek word meaning "instruct" which literally mean "to din into the ear."[88]

The *Catechumens* were of three grades or classes.[89]

- **i) Hearers** – They were permitted to listen to the reading of the scriptures and the sermons in the church. They were asked to learn elementary instructions in the fundamental doctrines and practices of the church. They should also continue learning by showing their way of conduct which helps them to be a worthy promotion for the second grade.
- **ii) Kneelers** – They remain for prayers after they were upgraded from the hearers. They also received more advanced instruction and had to prove by their manners of living.
- **iii) The Chosen** – They were given intensive doctrinal, liturgical, and ascetical training in preparation for baptism.

The bishops, the priests, and the deacons were the teachers. They gave full effort to meet the purpose of this school, to train

[87] Peter P. Person, *An Introduction to Christian Education* (Michigan: Baker Books, 1958), 24.

[88] Ellwood P. Cubberley, *The History of Education: Educational Practice and Progress Considered as a Phase of the Development and Spread of Western Civilization*, Kindle Edition (Boston: Houghton Mifflin, 1922), Location 1388.

[89] Eavey, *History of Christian Education*, 86–87.

morally and spiritually candidates for church membership. Their way of teaching is basically catechetical, i.e., by question and answer.

b. Catechetical School[90]

This school begins during the third century as a new type of Christian school. The purpose of this school was to equip the clergy with intellectual training equivalent to that of learned people of that day. This school produced Christian scholars who could think and reason like other educated people and had knowledge comparable to that possessed by teachers of Greco-Roman culture. During the time, *Alexandria's Catechetical* School was the most famous school founded by Mark gathering converts together for instructions. In 179 *Pantaenus*, a converter stoic philosopher became head of the school followed by Clement and Origen. Clement extended the curriculum which includes Greek literature, history, dialectic and science. He was known for his writings which made Greek learning and culture the handmaidens of Christianity. Origen rose to the highest point, attracting many pagans and Gnostic as well as Christians. It was told that until the 7th century Alexandria was the prominent centre of Christian thought.

4. Christian Education during Reformation Period

Reformation was very important it was within that context that various denominations and especially Methodist denomination came into being. Moreover, the Reformation constitutes a very critical period in the history of the Church, and in particular, that of Christian education. It characterizes the restoration of Christian doctrine, justification by faith, priesthood of all believers, etc., all of which have implications for Christian education. During the Reformation the content of Christian education was fully restored, the image of the Church brought to question, the beliefs and practices of the Roman Catholic Church out rightly challenged.

---

[90] Eavey, 88.

Reformation meant for Martin Luther, the purification of a corrupt institution.[91] Reformation had to do with the total turnaround of the Church in its teaching and practices. It is the renewal of the Church in doctrine, practice and emphasis. Like the Old and New Testament history of religious education, the Reformation also warrants special attention to practice, belief, and Christian living as it forms the basis on which Protestant Christian education came into being. Reformation directly impacted on the direction Christian education was to take from that time on.

Be that as it may, the middle Ages underscored the decline of Christian education. One can say Christian education was at its lowest ebb in terms of its limitation to monasteries, cathedral schools and universities, to the exclusion of masses. Celibacy or single life emerged as a viable option that redefined Christian faith[92] so that it was no longer faith in Jesus Christ alone, but it was all sorts of teachings which were to serve as provoking elements for the subsequent Reformation. The aim of the Reformation therefore was to restore true doctrine in the Church, especially the doctrine of salvation. Humanity is as it were, sinful before God and can only be made right with Him by believing in Jesus Christ.

Martin Luther and the reformers taught justification by faith and by grace alone; the earthly priest could therefore not mediate for anyone, nor could the buying of indulgences secure any form of forgiveness or release from purgatory.[93] Ulrich Zwingli was concerned about the nature of the Church; his goal was to engage in Biblical inquiry into the nature of the church and doctrine.[94] Moreover, the aim of the reformation was to ensure that the church returned to its former status of purity and preaching of pure doctrine. John

---

[91] James E Reed and Ronnie Prevost, *A History of Christian Education* (Nashville: Broadman Press, 1993), 189.

[92] Robert W. Pazmino, *Foundational Issues in Christian Education: An Introduction in Evangelical Perspective*, First Edition (Grand Rapids: Baker Academic, 1988), 131.

[93] Heiko A. Oberman, *Luther: Man between God and the Devil*, trans. Eileen Walliser Schwarzbart (New Haven: Yale University Press, 1982), 180.

[94] Robert C. Walton, "Huldrych Zwingli," ed. Donald K. McKim, *Encyclopedia of the Reformed Faith* (Edinburgh: Saint Andrew Press, 1992), 414.

Calvin maintained that the church needed to change, though it would be a costly undertaking.[95] For Desiderius Erasmus, what was of primary importance was Christlikeness.[96] To him this is all that really mattered. All in all, what reformers wanted to achieve was the preservation of a pure church through pure faith.[97]

E. The Meaning and Purpose of Christian Education

The meaning and the purpose of Christian education, is not as easy as it looks. One is bound to look into the concept of *'education'* itself as it has far reaching implications for Christian education. Further, other titles used for "Christian education" like "Religious Education", "Christian Religious Education", and "Holistic Christian Education" also come into play. These titles have to be explained and then relate to Christian education. It is only after this has been done that the purpose of Christian education can then be handled.

1. Meaning of Education

"Education" is a very broad concept. Consequently, different meanings have been attached to it. Several educationists and scholars have advanced the meaning of education from different contexts.

According to Thomas Groome, *Education* is an English word which comes from the Latin root, *educare,* meaning to lead out. The prefix "e" means 'out'. The root meaning of 'education' is thus, to lead out.[98]

Moran G, "Education either functions as an instrument which is used to facilitate the integration of the younger generation into the logic of the present system and bring about conformity to it, or it becomes the 'practice of freedom', the means by which men

---

[95] David Foxgrover, "Calvin as a Reformer: Christ's Standard-Bearer," in *Leaders of the Reformation*, ed. Richard L. DeMolen (London: Associated University Press, 1984), 80.

[96] Richard L. DeMolen, "Erasmus: Documents of Modern History," ed. Richard L. DeMolen (Edward Arnold, 1973), 15.

[97] Robert Ulich, *A History of Religious Education: Documents and Interpretations from the Judaeo-Christian Tradition* (New York: New York University Press, 1968), 107.

[98] Groome, *Christian Religious Education: Sharing Our Story and Vision*, 5.

and women deal critically and creatively with reality and discover how to participate in the transformation of their world."[99] In this particular case education is dealing critically and creatively with reality and discovery of how to participate. Education is not the means to anything else; it is the name of that constant reshaping or transforming in which embodied meaning 'e-merges' or is 'un-covered.'[100]

Admittedly, there are many definitions given as to what education is all about. It will not be possible to reflect all of them in this thesis. A brief analysis of the definitions given so far will be appropriate so as to reach some finality as to what education really is.

2. Meaning of Christian Education

Whereas it has been presumed, especially in western nations, that Christian education has to do with Christian faith, conversion and growth in that faith, it has become evident, however, that the term itself is ambiguous. It may mean four different things or even more.

First, Christian education can mean the kind of education Christians should engage in; that which Christians should know and be taught about, as opposed to general education intended for everyone else. In one sense, says Evelina Orteza Miranda, Christian education means the education or knowledge that a Christian should have as a Christian. It may not necessarily be Christian in outlook and content; it may be any subject for as long as it is something Christians should know about.[101] Rather, "there is a Christian perspective on it or a Christian manner of viewing it."[102] It is carried out in a Christian way.

---

[99] G. Moran, "Of a Kind and to a Degree: A Roman Catholic Perspective," in *Does the Church Really Want Religious Education: An Ecumenical Inquiry*, ed. M. Myer (Birmingham: Religious Education Press, 1988), 21.

[100] Moran, 21.

[101] E.O. Miranda, "Some Problems with the Expression 'Christian Education,'" in *Critical Perspectives on Christian Education: A Reader on the Aims, Principles and Philosophy of Christian Education*, ed. J. Astley and L.F. Francis (Herefordshire: Gracewing Fowler Wright Books, 1994), 20.

[102] Miranda, 17.

Second, Christian education may mean to others, "...the intellectual development of a critical evaluation of the Christian faith ..."[103] In this case one engages in the study of Christian faith critically. To this one can add the study of Christianity as a whole without really committing oneself to being a Christian. Such a focus would be on Christianity as a religion and on those who profess to be Christians.

Third, Christian education can mean to others, the whole approach to education. Jeff Astley points out that "Christian education" is a term that is also used to denote a reflective Christian perspective on the practice of general education, including education about religion, usually in the context of a school or higher education."[104] What this means is the critique of general education undertaken from a Christian perspective.

In the last instance, Christian education may, as it does in this thesis, mean the communication of God's truth (the Christian faith), with a view to making disciples of Christ. It has to do with conversion, nurture and service. It is the transmission of Christian faith to people so that they will believe and become followers of Christ, thereby living for Him and growing in Him to the point of serving Him in the world.

3. Concept of Holistic Christian Education

The researcher calls the understanding of Christian education a conventional one because many books that have been written on this subject assume this understanding. Moreover, the recent debate on what Christian education should mean, stems from the very fact that for a long time Christian education was understood to be concerned with Christian faith and nurture or discipleship.[105] Up until now,

---

[103] J. Astley, *The Philosophy of Christian Religious Education* (Birmingham: Religious Education Press, 1994), 14.

[104] J. Astley, "Definitions, Aims and Approaches: An Overview," in *Critical Perspectives on Christian Education: A Reader on the Aims, Principles and Philosophy of Christian Education*, ed. J. Astley and L.F. Francis (Herefordshire: Gracewing Fowler Wright Books, 1994), 4.

[105] The researcher understands discipleship to mean, the winning of unbelievers to Christ, the nurture of the new believers, the training and sending of the same

this is the understanding, and this does not however rule out the use of other terms for Christian education.

Against this background the researcher will now focus on the meaning of Christian education as it has evolved over time. The researcher will give several meanings from different educationists and authors; and then lift up what he considers to be important features or basic principles entailed in the term 'Christian education.'

Robert Pazmino defines Christian education as "...the deliberate, systematic and sustained divine and human effort to share or appropriate the knowledge, values, attitudes, skills, sensitivities and behaviours that comprise or are consistent with Christian faith. It fosters change, renewal and reformation of persons, groups and structures..."[106]

Randolph Crump Miller defines Christian education as "... the effort to make available for our generations – children, young people, and adults – the accumulated treasures of Christian life and thought, in such a way that God in Christ may carry on His redemptive work in each human soul and in the common life of man."[107]

"Christian education", says Lawrence Richards, "is concerned with life, and with growth of eternal life within the human personality, towards likeness to the God who gave it. Christian education is concerned with the progressive transformation of the behaviour toward the character, values, motives, attitudes, and understanding of God Himself...Christian education can never deal with individual life alone, it has to concern itself with the processes within the body which nurtures corporate and individual growth in Christ. Any Christian education approach which focuses on either...in the exclusion of the other is bound to fall short."[108] All

---

to do ministry. Discipleship embraces the whole of the Christian life: winning, building, training and serving.

[106] Pazmino, *Foundational Issues in Christian Education: An Introduction in Evangelical Perspective*, 88.

[107] Randolph Crump Miller, *Education for Christian Living* (New Jersey: Prentice Hall, 1956), 54.

[108] Lawrence Richards, *A Theology of Christian Education* (Grand Rapids: Zondervan, 1975), 16.

these definitions mentioned above connote directly or indirectly the holistic nature of the Christian education.

Researcher has described the meaning of Christian education, the titles often used for Christian education and the purpose of Christian education. Researcher intentional use of Holistic Christian education as a designation preferable to those already described, is without being opposed to the use of other titles like Christian education, Christian religious education, Religious education, etc., by other individuals. The features thus discussed, are very important as researcher attempts to deliberate holistic transformation of the congregation through Christian education among SMCI.

Brief Analysis of the Meanings mentioned: Five elements entailed in the process of Christian education are, teaching (transmission), winning, building, training, and sending or service.[109] Any definition of Christian education should have these five elements, though they may be expressed otherwise.

Admittedly, many other definitions have been advanced by countless other authors. The few mentioned are representative of the total picture portrayed by various authors. Researcher argues that Christian Education is the transmission (presentation) of Christian faith (the gospel, God's revelation) to people (individually and corporately) with a view to converting them to God (or to Christian faith) through Christ, nurturing them in Christian faith so they will grow or build intellectually, morally, socially, psychologically, and preparing them for ministry in the world, and ensuring that they carry out the ministry in the power of the Holy Spirit. Thus, the entire work of Christian education is holistic in nature, which can be termed as Holistic Christian education.

4. Purpose of (Holistic) Christian Education

Whatever purpose we may come up with must surely be in line with what Jesus, His disciples, and the early church did in the area of Christian education (Acts 4: 13; I John 2:6); their purpose must be

[109] Dumile Johannes Matshiga, "Christian Education in the Baptist Convention of South Africa with Special Reference to Churches in the Transvaal: A Practical Theological Investigation" (PhD Dissertation, University of Pretoria, 2001), 85.

our purpose. Methods, contexts and approaches may differ, but the purpose must be the same; it must be derived from Scriptures.

Robert Pazmino argues for conversion as a goal of Christian Education; conversion not understood as a once off event like Paul's conversion to faith on the road to Damascus. Pazmino refers to the kind of conversion that is continuous, so that it has proclamation, growth and maturity as well as ministry in it.[110]

Some aims are brief, for example, "*to bring all of man's experiences under the control of God*";[111] "*the man of God perfected in character and conduct until he is like God*";[112] "*to make men whole*";[113] "*...to produce godliness and Christ like maturity.*"[114] It will not be possible to reflect all interpretations of the purpose of Christian Education by different authors.

However, something about the purpose of Christian Education according to Jesus and Paul needs to be said. The purpose of Christian Education for Jesus and Paul was conversion (Matthew 6:33; John 3:3, 4; 6:28,29: Acts 17:1-5; Romans 10:1-4; I Thessalonians 1:9); spiritual growth and maturity (Matthew 5-7; 13; John 15; Acts 18:11; Ephesians 4: 11-15; Colossians 1:9-11); entry into heaven (Matthew 5:8; 7:21-25; 25; Luke 10:20) perfection of the saints for presentation before God (at the coming of Christ) (Colossians 1:28; I Thessalonians 5:23); strengthening of believers (Matthew 5-7; 24; John 14-1; Acts 14:22; I Thessalonians 3:2-4) and preparation of believers for ministry (service) (Mark 1: 17; Luke 10: 1-20; John 13; 15; 20:21; 21:15-17; Ephesians 4:11-12; II Timothy 2:2). Thus, we see the holistic nature of the ministry of Jesus and Paul, which has influenced the ministry of Christian education since its inception. The purpose of Christian education at the outset is complete transformation of the individual, church, community, and the society in general.

---

[110] Robert W. Pazmino, *Principles and Practices of Christian Education* (Grand Rapids: Baker Books, 1992), 38, 39.

[111] Eavey, *History of Christian Education*, 54.

[112] Eavey, 56.

[113] Miller, *Education for Christian Living*, 55.

[114] Gangel and Benson, *Christian Education: Its History and Philosophy*, 27.

F. Understanding Transformation

The concept of 'Transformation' may have a similar meaning as 'change' since many authors have used both terms interchangeably. H.G. Mithra opines that transformation can be either for good or for bad,[115] i.e., changing in a positive or a negative way. Thus, these two terms transformation and change can be attributed to either good or bad, and these terms are used simultaneously in the research study.

The Greek equivalent in the New Testament of what is commonly translated as "to transform" is the word *metamorpho*. *Metamorpho* occurs four times throughout the New Testament, twice in the Gospels and twice in the letters of Paul. The two occurrences in Paul's epistles, Romans 12:1-2 and 2 Corinthians 3:18, shall be considered, for they provide a clear outline of what transformation can look like in the lives of God's people.[116] The two occurrences of *metamorpho* in the Gospels are both found in the parallel radar of Jesus' transfiguration, namely in Mark 9:2 and Matthew 17:2.[117] Indeed, in these passages, the word *metamorpho* is not translated as "to transform," but rather "to transfigure."

Selvaraj A. defines transformation as "an overall change in the total being of a person or a community – educationally (intellectually), socially, psychologically, and economically and even culturally."[118] Change here refers to any modifications in the total individual, social organization of a society, in any of its institutions

[115] H.G. Mithra, "Christian Education: Agent of Liberation and Transformation," in *Becoming a Missional Congregation in the Twenty-First Century Indian Context*, ed. Jangkholam Haokip and Sungjemmeren K. Imchen (Delhi: ISPCK, 2016), 118.

[116] S. Steve Kang and Michael Feldman, "Transformed by the Transfiguration: Reflections on a Biblical Understanding of Transformation and Its Implications for Christian Education," *Christian Education Journal*, 3, 10, no. 2 (2013): 366.

[117] The transfiguration is also recorded in Luke 9:28-36. Interestingly, instead of using meta- morpho or other cognate verbs, Luke in v.29 uses an adjective, heteros (another in kind, different, or of 2), without supplying a verb.

[118] A. Selvaraj, *Christianity and Social Transformation: A Kerala Story* (Trivandrum: ICRO, 2002), 10.

or patterns of social roles.[119] Thanzauva cited B. Kuppuswamy who affirms that, transformation is a process of discernible and significant change in the form, structure, system, function and condition of an individual, community, and society.[120]

Mary Elizabeth Moore opines, that transformation is 'initiated by God's action', human beings are created with potentiality for self-improvement that requires responding to God's gift and call; and as a social being, and 'true humanity is realized only in relationship with others.'[121] This gives ample of support for the transformational vision of the Christian education.

At the outset, the definitions mentioned above clearly signifies that transformation is referred to all aspects of life. It cannot be complete without considering the moral, intellectual, and socio-cultural changes when compared to spiritual or faith transformation in the praxis of Christian education. Transformation is thus holistic.

G. Holistic Christian Education and Transformation

Human beings are created as holistic beings, and this creaturely reality has important implications for education. Humans are not mere "heads" to unlatch, open up, and pour content into; imparting knowledge is not enough.[122] The apostle Paul explained that "knowledge of the truth" through education never stands alone; it must always be "in accordance with godliness" (Titus 1:1). Such godliness involves the appropriation, development, and expression of sanctified thoughts, emotions, decisions, actions, motivations, and purposes.[123]

The draft on *Holistic Catechesis* of the Catechism for the Universal Church, prepared by the pontifical commission and intended to be

---

[119] B. Bhushan, ed., "Social Change," *Dictionary of Sociology* (New Delhi: Anmol Publications, 1989), 285.

[120] K. Thanzauva, *Transforming Theology: A Theological Basis for Social Transformation* (Bangalore: Asian Trading Corporation, 2002), 1.

[121] Mary Elizabeth Moore, *Education for Continuity and Change* (Nashville: Abingdon Press, 1983), 132.

[122] James R. Estep Jr., Michael J. Anthony, and Gregg R. Allison, *A Theology for Christian Education* (Nashville: B & H Academic, 2008), 189.

[123] Estep Jr., Anthony, and Allison, 189.

compendium of Catholic teaching, has sparked a heated debate among the bishops, theologians, and catechetical experts.[124] This document appealed for the balanced approach to catechesis or the religious instruction within the church that influences the transformation of the whole person. Relying primarily on the thoughts of Friedrich von Hugel and John Westerhoff regarding the nature of integral religious development, the approach presented here insists on the importance of the following two propositions:[125]

1. Religious development of the whole person requires not only an institutional element that transmits a body of beliefs to its members, but also a critical aspect that invites the reflective self-appropriation of conventional propositional faith and a mystical element that fosters personal religious experience (Friedrich von Hugel).
2. The process of catechesis or religious instruction includes the processes of formation, education, and instruction – each of these processes complementing each other in an effort to develop the whole person (John Westerhoff).

Schools bring transformation in the life of a student through education, the same way the holistic transformation is evident through Christian education. Unlike secular education, the precept of Christian education gives much importance on human values. However, the environment is quite threatened at times when the cherished values, morality and condition of lives are changed. Holistic Christian education desires to focus to transform the individual and society. In words of Allen J. Moore, "religious education is an ethical way of life that serves to transform religious platitudes into concrete social structures that are just and serve the welfare of all people."[126] To strengthen this, God's word must be known, understood, lived, and

[124] Au S.J. Wilkie, "Holistic Catechesis: Keeping Our Balance in the 1990s," *Religious Education* 86, no. 3 (Summer 1991): 347.

[125] Wilkie, 350.

[126] Allen J. Moore, "Book Review on Religious Education as Social Transformation," by Tecla Sund Reklau, *Christian Century* 106, no. 36 (November, 1989): 1125.

acted upon. Equipping an individual and groups for holistic action is possible through Christian education.[127] Therefore, Christian education must be brought in line with the holistic message of the gospel.

At the outset, Christian education and transformation are to be holistic. According to Simanga Kumalo, "the ultimate goal of (holistic approach to) Christian education should be the total (holistic) transformation of oppression to freedom, dehumanization to humanization, poverty to self-sufficiency, religious intolerance to religious tolerance."[128] Paulo Friere's idea in Samson Prabhakar words, humanization can be used to bring about a desired transformation in the Christian communities and in the society at large.[129] On the total personality transformation, Campbell Wyckoff affirms religious education as "the guided process to help a person achieve at each stage of their growth such as habits, skills, attitudes, appreciations, knowledge, ideas, and intensions; and achieve more integrated personality, competent and satisfying living in their social environment, and increasing cooperativeness with God and man."[130]

1. Role of Christian Education in the process of Holistic Transformation

The holistic education movement does not have a single source, a predominant proponent, or a major form or expression.[131] Holistic education is a philosophy of education based on the premise that each person finds identity, meaning, and purpose in life through connections to the community, to the natural world,

---

[127] John H. Westerhoff, *Tomorrow's Church: A Community of Change* (Waco, TX: Word Books, 1976), 106.

[128] Simanga R. Kumalo, "Southern African Sources for an Authentic Christian Education for Social Transformation," *Journal of Theology for Southern Africa* 122 (July 2005): 62.

[129] Samson Prabhakar, *Essay on Christian Education and Liturgy* (Bangalore: SATHRI, 2003), 121.

[130] Campbell D. Wyckoff, *The Task of Christian Education* (Philadelphia: The Westminster Press, n.d.), 18.

[131] Scot Forbes, "Values in Holistic Education," in *Education, Spirituality and the Whole Child* (Third Annual Conference, London: Roehampton Institute, 1996), 1.

and to humanitarian values such as compassion and peace. Holistic education aims to call forth from people an essential reverence for life and a passionate love for learning. Holism is the idea that all the properties of a given system in any field of study cannot be determined or explained by the sum of its component parts. Instead, the system as a whole determines how its parts behave.[132] A holistic way of thinking tries to encompass and integrate multiple layers of meaning and experience rather than defining human possibilities narrowly.

Accordingly, Holistic Christian education for transformation is the basic premise that education addresses the development of the intellectual, affective, aesthetic and spiritual aspects of a person.[133] The church should show interest in such education to help the members grow from the philosophy that they at all levels are uniquely valuable persons and should be educated to use their God-given capacities to become principled individuals, qualified for any position of life. Education for transformation has to begin at home where the basic values of redemptive discipline and mental and physical health are to be balanced with the importance of work.[134] Since early days, SMCI has embraced the philosophy that Christian education should be redemptive in nature, for the purpose of restoring human beings to the image of God (2 Corinthians 4:4).

Mental, physical, social, and spiritual health, intellectual development, and service to humanity form core values that are essential aspects of the SMCI's educational philosophy in Telangana & Andhra Pradesh. In the following ideas, the researcher would consider the different aspects of transformations through the holistic

---

[132] It is the theory that parts of a whole are in intimate interconnection, such that they cannot exist independently of the whole, or cannot be understood without reference to the whole, which is thus regarded as greater than the sum of its parts. Holism is often applied to mental states, language, and ecology. See, "Holism," *English Oxford Living Dictionaries*, https://en.oxforddictionaries.com/definition/holism. Accessed November 4, 2016.

[133] John P. Miller, *Education and the Soul: Toward a Spiritual Curriculum* (New York: Suny Publishers, 2000), 34–35.

[134] John P. Miller, *Education and the Soul: Toward a Spiritual Curriculum* (New York: Suny Publishers, 2000), 36.

approach to Christian education among the members (children, young, and adult) of the SMCI, which is the primary aim of this research study.

a. Spiritual Transformation

A definition of spiritual formation first begins with a focus on being "formed" and "transformed,"[135] that focuses on lifelong process of human obedience to God that takes place in the context of community.[136] Hughes Oliphant Old uses the term "spiritual transformation" to "spiritual formation" which originates from the Roman Catholic theology, "spirituality" is used within the Protestant traditions, but Calvinists have used "piety" to the term "spirituality."[137] Dallas Willard defines spiritual formation, "in Christ is the process whereby the inmost being of the individual (the heart, will, or spirit) takes on the quality or character of Jesus Himself."[138] Also, Robert Molholland defines it as "a process of being conformed to the image of Christ for the sake of others."[139]

i. Biblical Images of Christian Spiritual Transformation

Spiritual transformation is the primary task of the Christian education. The very nature of the church is reflected in the nature of God –*mission Dei* (mission of God). The mission of God for the church is established in the Great Commission – Mathew 28:19, when the church is faithful to her mission, lives are formed and transformed into the "image and likeness of Christ."[140] The Bible provides significant examples of the spiritual life. James Wilhoit

---

[135] Mark A. Maddix, "Spiritual Formation and Christian Formation," in *Christian Formation: Integrating Theology & Human Development*, ed. James R. Estep Jr. and Jonathan H. Kim (Nashville: B & H Academic, 2010), 240.

[136] Maddix, 242.

[137] Hughes Oliphant Old, "What Is Reformed Spirituality? Played Over Again Lightly," *Calvin Studies* 7 (1994): 67.

[138] Dallas Willard, *The Great Omission: A Reclaiming; Jesus' Essential Teaching on Discipleship* (San Francisco: Harper Collins, 2006), 53.

[139] M. Robert Molholland, *Invitation to a Journey: A Road Map for Spiritual Formation* (Downers Grove: InterVarsity Press, 1993), 12.

[140] Maddix, "Spiritual Formation and Christian Formation," 244.

summarizes these examples in three sets of images: nurture (agriculture, gardening, human growth, intimacy); the journey (race, battle, struggle); and death and resurrection (dying with Christ, being born again).[141] According to Wilhoit, these three images of nurture, journey, and death/resurrection capture the essential aspects of the spiritual transformation.[142]

ii. Teaching Bible for Spiritual Transformation

Jackie L. Smallbones believes the Bible is "useful for teaching, for reproof, for correction and for training in righteousness" (2 Timothy 3:16),[143] and therefore is an essential tool for living the holy life to which Christians are called. Eugene Peterson believes, "God both was and is active in Scripture";[144] thus, God still speaks and lives still change. According to Smallbones, the more and better teaching methods are applied in the transmission of the scripture the better the results would be in the form of transformation, this means not the teaching methods but the scripture that brings change.[145]

Bible teaching should lead people beyond relevant application to genuine encounters with God. The term transformation refers to radical change that comes from deep within the person. Such change is lasting, because, as Helen Moyle claims, it "takes us to a place that is different from the one at which we started and prompts change in us that is essentially spiritual."[146] Transformation, therefore, is both a goal – to become perfectly like Christ – and a process – the journey towards increasing perfection.[147]

At the outset, Christian education and development is the process of spiritual transformation. The goals of both Christian

[141] James C. Wilhoit, *Spiritual Formation as If the Church Mattered* (Grand Rapids: Baker Books, 2008), 19.

[142] Wilhoit, 22.

[143] Jackie L. Smallbones, "Teaching Bible for Transformation," *Christian Education Journal*, 3 & 4, no. 2 (2007): 293.

[144] Eugene H. Peterson, *Working with Angles* (Grand Rapids: William B. Eerdmans, 1987), 78.

[145] Smallbones, "Teaching Bible for Transformation," 294.

[146] Helen Moyle, "The Experience of Learning," *The Way* 37, no. 2 (1997): 113.

[147] Smallbones, "Teaching Bible for Transformation," 295.

education and spiritual transformation are the same: "to be shaped and formed into the image and likeness of Christ Jesus." Christian educators, pastors, and the church leaders should have the new sense of hopefulness about the impact spiritual.transformation has on their lives and the life of the church. As we become more like Christ, may we display His love and grace in service to God, others, and the world.

b. Socio-Cultural Transformation

Education is a double edged sword and both sides of it are capable of effecting remarkable changes. Education is known for its crucial role as a catalyst for socio-cultural development while at times it is an instrument for decline. Raths and others attest to this when they wrote: "In the last World War, millions of human beings were exterminated by a country which had been regarded as one of the most civilized and educated in the society/world."[148] The assertion by Raths and others speak volumes about the damage misappropriated education can cause. This is a situation where the educated were involved in one of the most dreadful mass undertakings in the society witnessed in history so far.

In this day and age, educated people have been responsible directly or indirectly for the challenges facing holistic development and the human cause. Some of the negative practices include deception, false witnesses, theft, sexual offences, alcohol and drug abuse, abuse of office, corruption, idolatry, among others.[149] L.S. Vygotsky's socio-cultural theory of human learning describes learning as a social process and the origination of human intelligence in society or culture. The major theme of Vygotsky's theoretical framework is that social interaction plays a fundamental role in the socio-cultural transformation.[150] Against this backdrop, it emerges that education

[148] Louis E. Raths, Merrill Harmin, and Sidney B. Simon, *Values and Teaching: Working with Values in the Classroom* (Columbus: Charles E Merrill Publishers, 1966), 19.

[149] Joseph Muyomi Mulaa, "Life Skills Education: A Model for Socio-Cultural Transformation," *African Ecclesial Review* 54, no. 3&4 (2012): 306.

[150] L.S. Vygotsky, "On Psychological Systems," in *The Collected Works of L. S. Vygotsky: Problems of the Theory and History of Psychology*, ed. R.W. Rieber and J.

without morality and devoid of God's knowledge is barren, this coincides with Whitehead's assertion that "a merely well-informed man (or woman) is the most useless borne on God's earth."[151] Thus, Christian education is the vital praxis of God's values and the sound human relationships in the process of the socio-cultural transformation. Socio-cultural transformation is intertwined with Political and Economic stability or transformation of an individual or the society in general. The below points emphasize these respective transformations.

i. Political Transformation

The Hebrew Bible contains a complex chronicle of the Kings of Israel and Judah, written over the course of many generations by authors whose relationships and intimacy with the rulers of the several kingdoms changed widely in both intimacy and respect, also a number of political currents appear in New Testament writings. Early Christians were described by Celsus as those who refused military service and would not accept public office, nor assume any responsibility for the governing of cities.[152] Origen confirms this description and adds that Christians do more for the good of the empire by forming an "army of piety" that prays for the well-being of the emperor and the safety of the empire.[153] Christians, when rightly informed and motivated, change their character of political conclusions. They bring the moral standards of God's kingdom into the civic realm and thereby become agents of His common grace – of His provision for those who believe as well as those who don't.

ii. Economic Transformation

Economic transformation is perhaps the most important aspect of societal transformation, given the fact that the market dominates the

---

Wollock, vol. 3 (New York: Plenum Press, 1930), 95.

[151] A.N. Whitehead, *The Aims of Education and Other Essays* (New York: The Free Press, 1967), 1.

[152] Robert Wilken, *The Christians as the Romans Saw Them* (New Haven: Yale University Press, 1984), 125.

[153] Wilken, 117.

agenda of our globalized world today. The Bible teaches very clearly that God desires "social and economic justice" especially for the poor and the oppressed, who are called 'the poor' in the Bible.[154] Whether the person or the community turns to Christ or not, we hope that each individual in the general public will have been empowered to become mature and responsible (not dependent) citizens who can make dignified and wise decisions for their individual and communal life (including to be for or against Christ). They would be active participants (not passive or marginalized spectators) in tackling issues that affect their lives and destinies in the light of God's Word.[155] One of the goals of Holistic Christian education should thus include social-cultural transformation which is intertwined with political and economic transformation.

c. Cognitive Transformation

From the inception of the church to the present, Christians have incessantly engaged in a comprehensive study to provide an accurate exposition of the intellect as it relates to the Christian education.[156] Here, in this section the researcher presents an overview of the relationship between the cognitive (which the researcher considers as psychological) development and Christian education.

In general, the cognitive divides into rational and relational dimensions – *Schema* and *thema*, respectively,[157] *schema* denotes mental form, shape, or figure[158] and *thema* denotes primary (non-derivative) element or property of mind or the function of the intellect.[159] Based on the schematic perspective Jean Piaget developed

---

[154] David S. Lim, "Curriculum for Economic Transformation," *William Carey International Development Journal* 2, no. 4 (Fall 2013): 5.

[155] Lim, 6.

[156] Jonathan H. Kim, "Intellectual Development and Christian Formation," in *Christian Formation: Integrating Theology & Human Development*, ed. James R. Estep Jr. and Jonathan H. Kim (Nashville: B & H Academic, 2010), 64.

[157] Kim, 64.

[158] Henry George Liddell and Robert Scott, *A Greek-English Lexicon* (Oxford: The Clarendon Press, 1968), 789.

[159] Liddell and Scott, 789.

the theory of cognitive development of the child through age 13,[160] and thematic perspective was used by Lev Vygotsky to formulate socio-cultural development theory.[161] Faith and intellect are in a complementary relationship with one another, understanding their interrelatedness will provide holistic picture of Christian spiritual and intellectual growth.[162] Christian educators based on the Piaget's and Vygotsky's theories proposed two opposing views of Christian formation: one group asserting the human as the object of thinking who is capable formulating faith analytically, while the other asserting the human as the subject of thinking who is under the influence of praxis-consciousness.[163]

Implications for Cognitive Transformation: As mentioned in the previous sections of this study, through the holistic approach to Christian education several implications for the educational ministry of the church can be derived. We cannot equate the intellectual development with the Christian education or the faith formation for it is obvious that faith is more than intellect.[164] The teaching or the pedagogy should be intellectually challenging. Teaching should aim at challenging the equilibration or balance in the mind of the student.

In order to promote holistic Christian formation, nurture, denoting holistic teaching, has to become a central methodology in the church and the school. This teaching should be on the dialogic

---

[160] Jean Piaget, *The Child and Reality: Problem of Genetic Psychology* (New York: Grossman, 1972); Jean Piaget, *The Psychology of the Child* (New York: Basic Books, 1969); Jean Piaget, *Genetic Epistemology* (New York: Columbia University Press, 1970).

[161] William Frawley, *Vygotsky and Cognitive Science: Language and the Unification of the Social and Computational Mind* (Cambridge: Harvard University Press, 1997), 89.

[162] Kim, "Intellectual Development and Christian Formation," 64.

[163] James W. Fowler, *Stages of Faith* (San Francisco: Harper & Row, 1981); David Elkind, *The Child and Society: Essays in Applied Child Development* (New York: Oxford University Press, 1979); Cynthia J. Neal, "A Parenting Style for Nurturing Christian Wisdom," in *Limning the Psyche: Explorations in Christian Psychology*, ed. R. Roberts and M. Talbot (Eugene, Oregon: Wipf and Stock, 2003), 165–85; M.M. Wilcox, *Developmental Journey* (Nashville: Abingdon Press, 1979).

[164] Kim, "Intellectual Development and Christian Formation," 90.

impartation of the whole knowledge – involving theory, practice, and critical reflection.[165] Teaching or the pedagogy under these perspectives mentioned above leads to transformation and growth of the intellect of the child or the adult, which will result in the holistic transformation of the individual into the image and likeness of Christ Jesus (Hebrews 12:2).

d. Moral Transformation

Morality is not a mono-dimensional concept but rather it is multidimensional. Based on the insights from theology and social sciences, Christian educators have presented morality as having three interrelated dimensions: cognitive, affective, and behavioural.[166] *Cognitive* or moral reasoning elements of morality have been described as moral judgements, choices, decisions, etc.[167] Moral *Affective* refers to the sense of valuing and character formation, addressing the emotional domain.[168] Finally, moral *behaviour* refers to moral actions – the behaviours of an ethical person.[169] Ethics are more than the mental process of our decisions; their scope includes affect and behaviour. Ethics and morality imply the presence of norms. For Christian educators, ethics and morality are not simply a human or societal product; rather, they are dependent on God, which endeavours to illustrate the nature of Christian ethics and morality.[170]

---

165 Kim, 93.

166 Catherine Stonehouse, "Moral Development," *Evangelical Dictionary of Christian Education* (Grand Rapids: Baker Books, 2002), 487.

167 Perry Downs, "Promoting Moral Growth and Development," in *Street Children* (California: MARC, 1997), 66.

168 Robert M. Cooper, "Moral Formation in the Parish Church," *Anglican Theological Review* 69, no. 3 (1987): 283.

169 David R. Krathwohl, Benjamin S. Bloom, and Bertram B. Masic, *Taxonomy of Educational Objectives: Handbook 2 - Affective Domain* (New York: Longmans, 1964), 180.

170 James R. Estep Jr., "Moral Development and Christian Formation," in *Christian Formation: Integrating Theology & Human Development*, ed. James R. Estep Jr. and Jonathan H. Kim (Nashville: B & H Academic, 2010), 143.

The development of morals and faith are intertwined in the Christian approaches to development, one can be moral without being Christian, but it is not possible to be a Christian without being moral. As Perry Downs comments, "the church has always been concerned with morality because it is an important consequence to faith."[171] Thus, the moral transformation of a believer is a vital aspect of Christian education.

Ministry for Moral Transformation: Peter Scharf identifies three approaches to facilitate moral transformation as *indoctrination*, *values clarification*, and *developmental moral education* favouring the last approach over others.[172] Without using all these approaches, each approach alone is insufficient to facilitate Christian moral transformation.[173] Downs speaks of the influence of involvement and participation in a just or moral community, such as the church or Christian institution.[174] In these contexts, moral relationships are formed and hence, are critical for the formation of moral values within oneself, others, church and society, and ultimately God.[175] The combination of these three approaches within the church context is perhaps the most comprehensive and promising means of facilitating moral transformation within the congregation.

2. Role of the Church in Holistic Transformation

Paul's letter to the Ephesians contains one of the clearest and most succinct descriptions of the purpose of the church. He says that God has chosen the church to administer His agenda for the reconciliation of all things and that it is through the church that God

---

171 Perry Downs, *Teaching for Spiritual Growth* (Grand Rapids: Zondervan, 1994), 95.

172 Peter Scharf, "Indoctrination, Values Clarification, and Developmental Moral Education as Educational Responses to Conflict and Change in Contemporary Society," in *Readings in Moral Education*, ed. Peter Scharf (Minneapolis: Winston Press, 1978), 20–25.

173 Estep Jr., "Moral Development and Christian Formation," 148.

174 Downs, "Promoting Moral Growth and Development," 75–76.

175 Thomas P. Wallace, "Values and Spirituality: Enriching Curriculum Development and Teaching/ Learning Processes for a New Millennium," *Journal of Christian Education* 43, no. 1 (May 2000): 44.

will demonstrate this, His manifold and eternal purpose (Ephesians 3:9-11 and Colossians 1:20). Redemption was completed on the cross, but God has given the church the task of administering the process of restoration until His return.

The outstanding implication of Paul's assertion is that the church is more important to the healing of human brokenness — hunger, sickness, political corruption, and economic injustice — than civil leaders, state governments, economic policy and development, or scientific advancement. God will use these and other modalities to advance His purpose, but the church holds the principle ordination for this supreme assignment.[176] The Christian churches are increasingly involved in these programmes, in one way or another. Traditionally, the Christian response to human need has been one of compassion; missionaries have taken the benefits of modernity to their fields of service in the form of schools, medicine, hospitals, agricultural techniques and the like.[177] However, the church cannot fulfil her role until it understands her significance, and equips and mobilizes individual members to purposefully represent God's holistic agenda in their respective worlds. The church must equip and disperse her people into every sector of society as premeditated advocates for the will of God being done where those members live and serve.

Conclusion

The notion of holistic transformation has been and continues to be an issue of longstanding interest and reflection in a variety of fields of study including, philosophy, psychology, sociology, education, and specifically Christian education. *Transformation*, in this chapter of research study, is premised on the fact that the coming of God into one's life impacts him or her *forever*. It involves the restoration of God's image in humankind. It is a reality where the flavor of God intensifies in our lives as the Spirit pours into us and transforms

[176] Bob Moffitt, "The Role of the Church," in *Holistic Mission* (Forum for World Evangelization - 2004, Pattaya, Thailand: Lausanne Committee for World Evangelization, 2004), 66, https://www.lausanne.org/wp-content/uploads/2007/06/LOP33_IG4.pdf. Accessed November 11, 2016.

[177] Wayne G Bragg, "Beyond Development to Transformation," *International Review of Mission* 73, no. 290 (April 1984): 153.

our nature, spirituality, morality, intellectual capabilities, and social relationships; thus, making us more like the Creator in whose image we are formed. Therefore, this chapter has categorically reviewed the previous literature with the biblical and historical perspectives in relation to the meaning, purpose, concept, and role of holistic Christian education toward the complete or total transformation of the churches/congregations that includes members from all spheres of ages and gender, and the role of the church in the process of transformation.

The next chapter will deal with the data collected for the research study, analyzing and interpreting the data in relation to the holistic Christian education toward the total transformation of the congregations of the SMCI.

Chapter 3

Processing of Data and Interpretations from Field Research

Introduction

In the previous chapter it was learnt that holistic transformation of the members of the congregations is the main aim of Christian education. It also informed the biblical, historical backgrounds, and meanings of Christian education along with various (holistic) transformations and the concept of holistic Christian education. Based on this understanding the researcher has developed the third chapter with data collection from the leaders and members of the SMCI.

This chapter has two sets of questionnaires 1) leaders[178] and 2) members. Firstly, the questionnaire of the leaders is taken into consideration, where there are totally 22 respondents. Secondly, the questionnaire of the members is analysed with 140 total respondents. Both these questionnaires have six areas of query in relation to transformation like, respondents' view of Christian education, cognitive/intellectual, psychological, socio-cultural, spiritual, and

[178] Leaders in this research study means the pastors and as well as leaders in SMCI.

holistic transformations. The total respondents of the both sets of questionnaires are 162.

A. General Profile of Leaders and Members

Table 1. To condense the surplus data collected, the researcher has given the general information of the respondents from the both sets of questionnaires in this table. This general information contains gender, educational and theological qualifications, age, ministry and Christian experiences of the respondents.

The abbreviations[179] are provided in the footnotes.

<table>
<tr><th rowspan="2">Sl. No</th><th rowspan="2" colspan="2">Profile</th><th colspan="3">P/L</th><th colspan="3">Members</th><th rowspan="2">TR</th><th rowspan="2">T %</th></tr>
<tr><th>Res</th><th>%</th><th>T</th><th>Res</th><th>%</th><th>T</th></tr>
<tr><td>a</td><td rowspan="2">G</td><td>Male</td><td>18</td><td>81.8%</td><td rowspan="2">22</td><td>64</td><td>45.7%</td><td rowspan="2">140</td><td rowspan="2">162</td><td rowspan="2">100%</td></tr>
<tr><td>b</td><td>Female</td><td>4</td><td>18.2%</td><td>76</td><td>54.3%</td></tr>
<tr><td>a</td><td rowspan="4">SE</td><td>UM</td><td>-</td><td>-</td><td rowspan="4">22</td><td>24</td><td>17.2%</td><td rowspan="4">140</td><td rowspan="4">162</td><td rowspan="4">100%</td></tr>
<tr><td>b</td><td>AM</td><td>4</td><td>18.2%</td><td>82</td><td>58.5%</td></tr>
<tr><td>c</td><td>GR</td><td>-</td><td>-</td><td>-</td><td>-</td></tr>
<tr><td>d</td><td>PG</td><td>18</td><td>81.8%</td><td>34</td><td>24.3%</td></tr>
<tr><td>a</td><td rowspan="4">TE</td><td>NTB</td><td>10</td><td>45.5%</td><td rowspan="4">22</td><td>n/a</td><td>n/a</td><td rowspan="4">n/a</td><td rowspan="4">22</td><td rowspan="4">100%</td></tr>
<tr><td>b</td><td>C/D</td><td>2</td><td>9.1%</td><td>n/a</td><td>n/a</td></tr>
<tr><td>c</td><td>B.Th-B.D</td><td>8</td><td>36.4%</td><td>n/a</td><td>n/a</td></tr>
<tr><td>d</td><td>M.Th.</td><td>2</td><td>9.1%</td><td>n/a</td><td>n/a</td></tr>
</table>

[179] **P/L** – Leaders, **Res** – Respondents, **%** - Percentage, **T** – Total, **TR** – Total number of Respondents, **T%** - Total Percentage, **G** – Gender, **GR** – Graduation, **SE** – Secular Education, **TE** – Theological Education, **A** – Age, **ME/CE** – Ministerial Experience of P/L and Christian Experience of Members, **UM** – Under Matriculation, **AM** – Above Matriculation, **PG** – Post Graduation, **NTB** – Non-Theological Background, **C/D** – Certificate/Diploma Level Education, **n/a** – Not Applicable, **B.Th** – Bachelor of Theology, **B.D.** – Bachelor of Divinity, **M.Th** – Master of Theology.

<table>
<tr><td>a</td><td rowspan="4">A</td><td>20-30 yrs</td><td>2</td><td>9.1%</td><td rowspan="4">22</td><td>64</td><td>45.7%</td><td rowspan="4">140</td><td rowspan="4">162</td><td rowspan="4">100%</td></tr>
<tr><td>b</td><td>30-40yrs</td><td>2</td><td>9.1%</td><td>29</td><td>20.8%</td></tr>
<tr><td>c</td><td>40-50yrs</td><td>8</td><td>36.4%</td><td>35</td><td>25%</td></tr>
<tr><td>d</td><td>50>yrs</td><td>10</td><td>45.5%</td><td>12</td><td>8.5%</td></tr>
<tr><td>a</td><td rowspan="4">ME/ CE</td><td><3 yrs</td><td>2</td><td>9.1%</td><td rowspan="4">22</td><td>13</td><td>9.3%</td><td rowspan="4">140</td><td rowspan="4">162</td><td rowspan="4">100%</td></tr>
<tr><td>b</td><td>2-8 yrs</td><td>4</td><td>18.2%</td><td>4</td><td>2.8%</td></tr>
<tr><td>c</td><td>8-10 yrs</td><td>2</td><td>9.1%</td><td>12</td><td>8.6%</td></tr>
<tr><td>d</td><td>10> yrs</td><td>14</td><td>63.6%</td><td>111</td><td>79.3%</td></tr>
</table>

This table analyses shows that there are 81.8% of the male majority from leaders and 54.3% of female respondents in members' questionnaire. In secular education category among the leaders there are majority of post-graduates with 81.8% and among the members 58.5% are with above matriculation. 45.5% of leaders are without proper theological background followed by 36.4% of B.D. graduates.[180] Age was also calculated and found that 45.5% of the leaders are 50 years and above and from members 20 to 30 years of them lead the table with 46.6%. The ministerial experience of leaders and Christian experience of members were analysed, where most of them have more than 10 years of experience with 63.6% and 83.6% respectively. Thus, the analysis shows that the respondents' background is comprehensive in regard to education, age, Christian experience, and ministerial experience, which makes the empirical study viable towards findings of the hypothesis.

B. Leaders Questionnaire Analysis and Interpretation

In this section there are few tables where the researcher had combined with similar questions from the leaders' and members' questionnaires in order to condense the enormous data.

[180] The respondents here are both pastors with theological background and leaders without theological background in SMCI.

1. Leaders' Views on Christian Education

Table 2. Pastor/leader is responsible for Christian education

Sl. No.	Options	P/L Respondents	Percentage
a	To great extent	18	81.8%
b	To some extent	4	18.2%
c	No	-	-
Total		22	100%

According to table 2, majority of respondents (81.8%) agree to great extent that leaders in the church are responsible for sound impartation of Christian education, and the rest agree it to some extent. In general, it is assumed that Christian education is the responsibility of Sunday school teachers only and not the leaders of the church.

Table 3. As a pastor and member do you recommend Christian education?

Sl. No.	Options	Leaders		Members	
		Res-pondents	Per-centage	Respondents	Percentage
a	To great extent	20	90.9%	114	81.4%
b	To some extent	2	9.1%	8	5.8%
c	No	-	-	-	-
d	Not sure	-	-	18	12.8%
Total		22	100%	140	100%

The majority of respondents, i.e., 90.9% leaders and 81.4% members in table 3, agree that they would recommend rigorous Christian education ministry in the church settings.

Table 4. A pastor or a teacher should be transformed spiritually first

Sl.No.	Options	P/L Respondents	Percentage
a	Yes	22	100%
b	To some extent	-	-
c	Any other	-	-
Total		22	100%

Total respondents that is 100% of leaders believe that pastor or a teacher should first be transformed spiritually prior to his/her transformational ministry towards others as illustrated in table 4. Without, one being transformed, he/she cannot assume the transformation of others.

Table 5. Target audience of Christian education

Sl. No.	Options	Leaders		Members	
		Respondents	Percentage	Respondents	Percentage
a	Children	2	9.1%	16	11.4%
b	Youth	2	9.1%	12	8.6%
c	Adult	-	-	5	3.6%
d	All Inclusive	18	81.8%	107	76.4%
Total		22	100%	140	100%

The majority of leaders and members that is 81.8% and 76.4% respectively as analysed in table 5 suggests that everyone in the church are beneficiaries of Christian education that includes children, youth, and adults irrespective of gender.

Table 6. How do you educate believers into maturity in Christ?

Sl. No.	Options	Leaders		Members	
		Respondents	Percentage	Respondents	Percentage
a	Preaching & Teaching	12	54.6%	103	73.6%
b	Discipleship	10	45.4%	37	26.4%
Total		22	100%	140	100%

The data in table 6 depicts that majority of leaders (54.5%) and members (73.6%) agree that preaching and teaching as *modus operandi* of transmitting education to the believers. It is also to be noted that discipleship program is also acknowledged by few.

Table 7. Bible emphasises Christian education

Sl. No.	Options	P/L Respondents	Percentage
a	Nowhere it is mentioned in the Bible	2	9.1%
b	Bible is the basis for Christian education	18	81.8%
c	No idea	2	9.1%
Total		22	100%

Bible emphasises Christian education – majority of the respondents (81.8%) agree to this statement as per table 7. The main content of Christian education is the Bible, which is the foundation for developing curriculum for Christian education.

Table 8. In your opinion Christian education in your church is

Sl. No.	Options	P/L Respondents	Percentage
a	Intellectual/Cognitive Development	2	9.1%
b	Spiritual/Psychological Transformation	4	18.2%
c	Socio-Political Transformation	-	-
d	All Inclusive	16	72.7%
Total		22	100%

According to table 8, aim of Christian education is all inclusive or the holistic transformation is what 72.7% respondents agree. All inclusive here means holistic aspect that are spiritual, intellectual, social and moral transformations.

Table 9. The above transformations are possible through Christian education

Sl. No.	Options	P/L Respondents	Percentage
a	To great extent	14	63.6%
b	To some extent	8	36.4%
c	No	-	-
d	No idea	-	-
Total		22	100%

As shown in table 9, majority of respondents (63.6%) agree that all the transformations as mentioned in previous table (8) are possible through Christian education. Thus, Christian education is the source for holistic transformation.

Table 10. Do you aim at holistic transformation in your ministry?

Sl..No.	Options	P/L Respondents	Percentage
a	To great extent	18	81.8%
b	To some extent	4	18.2%
c	No	-	-
d	No idea	-	-
Total		22	100%

Most of the leaders that is 81.8% of them aim at holistic transformation in their ministry to the church members as shown in table 10. Holistic transformation is not evident in the congregation of SMCI despite of giving much importance to the same.

Table 11. Christian education is foundation for the holistic transformation

Sl. No.	Options	Leaders		Members	
		Respondents	Percentage	Respondents	Percentage
a	To great extent	18	81.8%	106	75.7%
b	To some extent	4	18.2%	19	13.6%
c	No	-	-	3	2.1%
d	Not sure	-	-	12	8.6%
Total		22	100%	140	100%

Based on the analysis of table 11, 81.8% of leaders and 75.5% of members agree that Christian education is the foundation for holistic transformation of the congregation. Generally, the church consider that Christian education is meant for spiritual transformation.

Table 12. Consistency with aims and objectives of Christian education

Sl.No.	Options	P/L Respondents	Percentage
a	To great extent	18	81.8%
b	Some extent	4	18.2%
c	No	-	-
d	No idea	-	-
Total		22	100%

When inquired about the ministry's consistency with Christian education's aim and objectives, table 12 points to the majority of the respondents (81.8%) agree that ministry of the leaders is persistent with aims and objectives.

Table 13. Christian education helps members grow in Biblical knowledge

Sl. No.	Options	Leaders		Members	
		Respondents	Percentage	Respondents	Percentage
a	To great extent	20	90.9%	117	83.6%
b	To some extent	2	9.1%	13	9.3%
c	No	-	-	4	2.8%
d	No idea	-	-	6	4.3%
Total		22	100%	140	100%

According to table 13, 90.9% of leaders and 83.6% of members agree to a great extent that Christian education helps the members of the congregations grow in Biblical knowledge.

Table 14. Christian education builds strong cognitive/ intellectual capabilities

Sl.No.	Options	P/L Respondents	Percentage
a	Certainly	22	100%
b	Doubtful	-	-
c	Any other	-	-
Total		22	100%

100% of the respondents in the above table agree that intellectual and cognitive capabilities of learners will improve through Christian education. Therefore, the leadership of SMCI is aware of Christian education's role in intellectual development of the members.

Table 15. Christian education helps in spiritual and psychological development

Sl. No.	Options	Leaders		Members	
		Respondents	Percentage	Respondents	Percentage
a	To great extent	22	100%	118	84%
b	To some extent	-	-	14	10%
c	No	-	-	6	4.8%
d	No idea	-	-	2	1.2%
Total		22	100%	140	100%

All the leaders (100%) and majority of members (84%) agree to a great extent that spiritual and psychological development is possible through the impartation of Christian education according to table 15.

Table 16. Christian education brings awareness in social and cultural areas

Sl. No.	Options	P/L Respondents	Percentage
a	To great extent	16	72.7%
b	Sometimes	6	27.3%
c	No	-	-
d	No idea	-	-
Total		22	100%

Majority of respondents (72.7%) in table 16 believe that Christian education brings awareness in social and cultural areas. Not only spiritual and intellectual development but also socio-cultural transformation is possible through Christian education.

Table 17. Christian education inspires for holistic transformation

Sl. No.	Options	Leaders		Members	
		Respondents	Percentage	Respondents	Percentage
a	Yes	20	90.9%	110	78.6%
b	Rarely	2	9.1%	20	14.3%
c	No	-	-	2	1.4%
d	No idea	-	-	8	5.7%
Total		22	100%	140	100%

As per table 17 majority of leaders and members that is 90.9% and 78.6% respectively agree that Christian education informs, invites, and inspires people for holistic transformation.

2. Cognitive or Intellectual Transformation

Table 18. Do you know intellectual capabilities of the members in the church?

Sl. No.	Options	Leaders		Members	
		Respondents	Percentage	Respondents	Percentage
a	Yes	14	63.6%	90	64.4%
b	To some extent	8	36.4%	42	30%
c	No	-	-	4	2.8%
d	Not needed	-	-	4	2.8%
	Total	22	100%	140	100%

Majority of leaders (63.6%) and members (64.4%) are aware of the intellectual capabilities of members in the church according to table 18. This table also explains that few leaders and members are aware of intellectual abilities of members to some extent.

Table 19. Need of intellectual believers who are analytical & logical

Sl. No.	Options	Leaders		Members	
		Respondents	Percentage	Respondents	Percentage
a	Many are needed	16	72.7%	82	58.6%
b	Few are needed	6	27.3%	50	35.8%
c	No	-	-	4	2.8%
d	Have no idea	-	-	4	2.8%
	Total	22	100%	140	100%

According to table 19, 72.7% leaders and 58.6% members believe that there is a need of many intellectual believers in the church who are analytical and logical in their understanding of the words and actions.

Table 20. Recommend/participate in scholarly teachings/ lectures

Sl. No.	Options	Leaders		Members	
		Respondents	Percentage	Respondents	Percentage
a	To great extent	14	63.6%	90	64.3%
b	To some extent	8	36.4%	44	31.5%
c	No	-	-	4	2.8%
d	No idea	-	-	2	1.4%
Total		22	100%	140	100%

The majority of respondents from leaders (63.3%) and members (64.3%) recommend members to participate in scholarly/academic lectures in church settings as it is an important factor for the intellectual development of the members in SMCI according to table 20.

Table 21. Members to read books and materials apart from the Bible

Sl. No.	Options	Leaders		Members	
		Respondents	Percentage	Respondents	Percentage
a	Yes	14	63.6%	67	47.9%
b	Rarely	8	36.4%	63	45%
c	No	-	-	6	4.3%
d	Not thought of	-	-	4	2.8%
Total		22	100%	140	100%

According to the above table which is combined question 26 from leaders' and question 24 from members' questionnaires disclose that 63.6% of leaders and 47.9% of members recommend not only the Bible but also various books and materials should be made available to the believers and motivate them to read.

Table 22. Members are capable of defending their faith and practices

Sl.No.	Options	P/L Respondents	Percentage
a	Yes	14	63.6%
b	Not everybody	8	36.4%
c	Not sure	-	-
Total		22	100%

The inquiry in table 22 show that majority of respondents that is 63.6% agree that the members of the church are capable of defending their faith and practices intellectually. However, 36.4% of them believe that not everybody is capable of defending faith intellectually.

Table 23. Strive to develop the members' intellectual abilities

Sl. No.	Options	Leaders		Members	
		Respondents	Percentage	Respondents	Percentage
a	To great extent	12	54.5%	80	57.2%
b	To some extent	10	45.5%	39	27.9%
c	No	-	-	15	10.7%
d	Not sure	-	-	6	4.2%
	Total	22	100%	140	100%

The majority of leaders and members that is 54.5% and 57.2%, respectively, assert that they strive to develop the intellectual abilities of the members through the ministry of Christian education according to table 23.

Table 24. Ministry method to all age groups in the church are similar

Sl. No.	Options	Leaders		Members	
		Respondents	Percentage	Respondents	Percentage
a	Yes	12	54.5%	68	48.6%
b	Sometimes	4	18.2%	42	30%
c	No	6	27.3%	25	17.8%
d	No Idea	-	-	5	3.6%
Total		22	100%	140	100%

The majority of respondents from members (48.6%) and leaders (54.5%) as in table 24, agree that the same ministry methods are being used by the leaders to all the age groups in the church. In addition to this, leaders deal all age groups at the same level. Therefore, they do not have the understanding of the developmental stages of an individual.

Table 25. Does your teaching/preaching includes intellectual nurture

Sl. No.	Options	Leaders		Members	
		Respondents	Percentage	Respondents	Percentage
a	Yes	18	81.8%	80	57.2%
b	To some level	4	18.2%	52	37.2%
c	No	-	-	4	2.8%
d	No Idea	-	-	4	2.8%
Total		22	100%	140	100%

The above table is combined with question 30 from pastors' and question 28 from members' questionnaires. The respondents were asked whether preaching and teaching ministry of leaders includes intellectual nurture along with spiritual enlightenment. As a response, 81.8% of leaders and 57.2% of members have agreed that they do so.

Table 26. Members maturing in the church's traditions, teachings, and practices

Sl. No.	Options	Leaders		Members	
		Respondents	Percentage	Respondents	Percentage
a	Yes	16	72.7%	70	50.0%
b	Most of the time	6	27.3%	48	34.3%
c	Very few	-	-	14	10%
d	No	-	-	8	5.7%
	Total	22	100%	140	100%

Most of the leaders and members that is 72.7% and 50% respectively as analysed in table 26 reveal that many members are growing toward maturity of the church's traditions, teachings, and practices. Here, tradition or practices of the church does not mean denominational but the church as the Body of Christ.

Table 27. Members helpful in the ministry to other members

Sl. No.	Options	Leaders		Members	
		Respondents	Percentage	Respondents	Percentage
a	Yes	16	72.7%	100	71.4%
b	Few of them	6	27.3%	6	4.3%
c	Depends on the situation	-	-	30	21.4%
d	No	-	-	4	2.9%
	Total	22	100%	140	100%

According to table 27 which is a combination of question 32 from leaders' and question 30 from the members' questionnaires, 72.7% of leaders and 71.4% of members agree that the congregation members are being helpful to the pastor or leader in the ministry of the church.

3. Psychological Transformation

Table 28. Do you understand psychological levels of the church members?

Sl. No.	Options	Leaders		Members	
		Respondents	Percentage	Respondents	Percentage
a	Yes	14	63.6%	102	72.9%
b	To some extent	8	36.4%	30	21.4%
c	No	-	-	2	1.4%
d	No Idea	-	-	6	4.3%
	Total	22	100%	140	100%

Most of the leaders (63.6%) and members (72.9%) state that they understand the psychological levels of church members according to table 28. This indicates that the respondents are aware of psychological levels or developmental stages of the church members.

Table 29. Psychology provides answers to the human mental condition

Sl. No.	Options	Leaders		Members	
		Respondents	Percentage	Respondents	Percentage
a	Yes	4	18.2%	80	57.2%
b	To some extent	12	54.5%	16	11.4%
c	No	4	18.2%	44	31.4%
d	Not sure	2	9.1%	-	-
	Total	22	100%	140	100%

The majority of leaders that is 54.5% agree to some extent that psychology has the answers to the human mental condition and play important role in living a better life, but 57.2% of members agree to a great extent that psychology has the answers for human conditions as per table 29.

Table 30. A pastor should know the basics of psychology for a better ministry

Sl.No.	Options	P/L Respondents	Percentage
a	Yes	14	63.6%
b	To some extent	6	27.3%
c	No	-	-
d	Can't say	2	9.1%
Total		22	100%

The above table emphasises the basic knowledge of psychology in pastoral ministry. 63.6% leaders agree that a pastor should know the basics of psychology. A basic knowledge of Psychology plays a vital role in the life and ministry of a pastor.

Table 31. Psychological understanding is essential for faith formation

Sl. No.	Options	Leaders		Members	
		Respondents	Percentage	Respondents	Percentage
a	Yes	14	63.6%	86	61.4%
b	To some extent	6	27.3%	-	-
c	No	-	-	10	7.2%
d	Not sure	2	9.1%	44	31.4%
Total		22	100%	116	100%

63.6% of leaders and 61.4% of members agree that psychology is essential for faith formation, thus, a pastor should know the basics of psychology to impart Christian education according to table 31. Thus, psychology plays an important role in faith formation.

Table 32. Do you adopt psychological theories in Christian educational ministry?

Sl. No.	Options	Leaders		Members	
		Respondents	Percentage	Respondents	Percentage
a	Yes	6	27.3%	48	34.3%
b	Sometimes	10	45.5%	50	35.7%
c	No	6	27.3%	18	12.9%
d	No idea	-	-	24	17.1%
Total		22	100%	140	100%

According to the analysis in the above table 32 that discusses about the psychological theories and their role in the Christian education ministry, to which 45.5% leaders and 35.7% members agree that these theories are adopted on some occasions in the ministry. Thus, this table shows, these theories are not utilized extensively.

Table 33. Psychology brings awareness in emotions to bring closer to God

Sl. No.	Options	Leaders		Members	
		Respondents	Percentage	Respondents	Percentage
a	To great extent	10	45.5%	70	50%
b	To some extent	10	45.5%	29	20.7%
c	Not at all	-	-	16	11.4%
d	May be	2	9%	25	17.9%
Total		22	100%	140	100%

The majority of the leaders (45.5%) and members (50%) believe to a great extent that psychology deals with human emotions. In that psychology can be used in bringing an individual closer to God according to table 33. There are also equal respondents from leaders who believe that psychology transpires to some extent.

Table 34. Psychology could provide practical techniques for Christian education

Sl.No.	Options	P/L Respondents	Percentage
a	Yes	14	63.6%
b	Very rare	6	27.3%
c	Any other	2	9.1%
Total		22	100%

63.6% of leaders state that psychology has a vital role to play in developing techniques in pedagogy according to table 34. Practical techniques for imparting Christian education can be supported by the developmental stages of the learner, which is possible through psychology.

Table 35. Bible has answers for any issue related to psychological problems

Sl. No.	Options	Leaders		Members	
		Respondents	Percentage	Respondents	Percentage
a	To great extent	18	81.8%	84	60%
b	To some extent	2	9.1%	24	17.2%
c	No	2	9.1%	28	20%
d	Not sure	-	-	4	2.8%
Total		22	100%	140	100%

Most of the respondents from leaders (81.8%) and members (60%) agree to a great extent that the Bible has the information about the psychological problems faced by people, which can be used to impart Christian education. This reveals that the majority of leaders and members realize Bible has ample of examples in relation to psychological issues among the humans.

4. Socio–Cultural Transformation

Table 36. Is it viable to give importance to Social and Cultural awareness?

Sl. No.	Options	Leaders		Members	
		Respondents	Percentage	Respondents	Percentage
a	Certainly	16	72.7%	106	75.8%
b	To some extent	4	18.2%	26	18.6%
c	No	2	9.1%	4	2.8%
d	Not sure	-	-	4	2.8%
Total		22	100%	140	100%

The above table discusses about the viability given to social and cultural awareness by the Christian educators that can help in bringing social and cultural transformation, to which 72.7% of leaders and 75.8% of members presume it is certainly needed. Christian education generally is thought of being only spiritual. On the other hand, for some it includes intellectual/psychological and moral transformations. In addition to this, socio-cultural is as important as any other transformation.

Table 37. Socio-Cultural view is changed through Christian education

Sl. No.	Options	Leaders		Members	
		Respondents	Percentage	Respondents	Percentage
a	Yes	18	81.8%	90	64.3%
b	To some extent	4	18.2%	46	32.9%
c	No	-	-	2	1.4%
d	Not sure	-	-	2	1.4%
Total		22	100%	140	100%

Socio-cultural understanding of an individual can be changed through the impartation of Christian education. 81.8% of leaders and 64.3% of members agree with this view according to table 37. Certainly, Christian education brings changes in socio-cultural view.

Table 38. The social relationships are developed through Christian education

Sl. No.	Options	Leaders		Members	
		Respondents	Percentage	Respondents	Percentage
a	To great extent	18	81.8%	101	72.2%
b	To some extent	4	18.2%	29	20.8%
c	No	-	-	6	4.2%
d	Not idea	-	-	4	2.8%
Total		22	100%	140	100%

81.8% of leaders and 72.2% of members according to table 38 consider to a great extent that Christian education ministry emphasizes and also transforms an individual for better social relationships with the people outside the church.

Table 39. Christian education brings social change

Sl. No.	Options	Leaders		Members	
		Respondents	Percentage	Respondents	Percentage
a	To great extent	14	63.6%	110	78.7%
b	To some extent	8	36.4%	22	15.7%
c	No	-	-	4	2.8%
d	Have no idea	-	-	4	2.8%
Total		22	100%	140	100%

Christian education brings social change. 63.6% of leaders and 78.7% of members agree to this opinion to a great extent as analysed in table 39. Therefore, Christian education has a great role in bringing social changes. Social change can be towards positive or negative change.

Table 40. Cultural transformation is the work of individuals

Sl.No.	Options	P/L Respondents	Percentage
a	Yes	10	45.5%
b	To some extent	4	18.2%
c	No	6	27.3%
d	May be	2	9.1%
Total		22	100%

According to table 40, 45.5% respondents resolve that every individual in the local church has the responsibility of cultural transformation of the other members. Adapting to cultural diversities and transforming oneself accordingly is the obligation of every individual not just the local church.

Table 41. Christian education also brings awareness in cultural diversities

Sl. No.	Options	Leaders		Members	
		Respondents	Percentage	Respondents	Percentage
a	To great extent	14	63.6%	110	78.6%
b	To some extent	6	27.3%	22	15.7%
c	No	-	-	6	4.3%
d	Not sure	2	9.1%	2	1.4%
Total		22	100%	140	100%

63.6% of leaders and 78.6% of members agree that Christian education brings awareness in cultural diversities to a great extent as per table 41. The impartation of Christian education should be done in such a way where members under the cultural diversities, adapt it to their lifestyle accordingly.

Table 42. Is there any relationship of socio-cultural and economic transformation?

Sl. No.	Options	Leaders		Members	
		Respondents	Percentage	Respondents	Percentage
a	Yes	14	63.6%	96	68.6%
b	To some extent	6	27.3%	32	22.9%
c	No	-	-	4	2.8%
d	No idea	2	9.1%	8	5.7%
Total		22	100%	140	100%

The majority of respondents according to table 42, 63.6% of leaders and 68.6% of members agree that there is a relationship between socio-cultural transformation and economic transformation. Social and cultural relationships are developed based on the economic background of an individual. Christian education helps an individual to strike a balance between his/her own economic background and the respective social relationships.

Table 43. Christian education can bring awareness on economies of the people

Sl. No.	Options	Leaders		Members	
		Respondents	Percentage	Respondents	Percentage
a	Yes	**20**	**90.9%**	**116**	**82.9%**
b	Rarely	2	9.1%	10	7.1%
c	No	-	-	4	2.9%
d	May be	-	-	10	7.1%
Total		22	100%	140	100%

90.9% leaders and 82.9% of members are confident that Christian education helps people in managing the economies of the members, like being content, stewardship, accountability, etc., according to table 43, and these should be included in the curriculum of Christian education as well.

Table 44. One of the main concerns of Christian education is social justice

Sl. No.	Options	Leaders		Members	
		Respondents	Percentage	Respondents	Percentage
a	Yes	14	63.6%	90	64.3%
b	To some extent	6	27.3%	20	14.2%
c	No	-	-	4	2.9%
d	Not sure	2	9.1%	26	18.6%
Total		22	100%	140	100%

The majority of leaders (63.6%) and members (64.3%) suggest that one of the main concerns of Christian education is social justice as per the analysis in table 44. This is one of the important aspects of this research. Christian education is concerned with social justice. This justice is possible when people are socio-culturally transformed.

5. Spiritual Transformation

Table 45. Faith formation is emphasized in the teaching and learning process

Sl. No.	Options	Leaders		Members	
		Respondents	Percentage	Respondents	Percentage
a	To great extent	22	100.0%	120	85.7%
b	Very rare	-	-	3	2.1%
c	No	-	-	6	4.3%
d	No idea	-	-	11	7.9%
Total		22	100%	140	100%

100% leaders and 85.7% members agree to a great extent that faith formation is emphasized in teaching and learning praxis within the church settings according to table 45. It is generally understood that impartation of Christian education is a process in which Christian faith is transmitted into the lives of the people.

Table 46. Approximate maturity level of faith among the believers

Sl. No.	Options	Leaders		Members	
		Respondents	Percentage	Respondents	Percentage
a	High	6	27.3%	56	40%
b	Medium	10	45.5%	55	39.5%
c	Low	6	27.3%	25	17.6%
d	No idea	-	-	4	2.9%
Total		22	100%	140	100%

There is a variation of opinions in relation to the spiritual maturity level of members, 45.5% leaders and 39.5% members believe that members' spirituality level is to medium or average, as per the above table. This discloses that the Christian education is not appealing to the spiritual development of individuals, even though many believe Christian education is related to spirituality.

Table 47. Members discover spiritual truths on their own

Sl. No.	Options	Leaders		Members	
		Respondents	Percentage	Respondents	Percentage
a	Yes	16	72.7%	58	41.4%
b	To some extent	6	27.3%	68	48.6%
c	No	-	-	8	5.3%
d	Don't know	-	-	6	4.7%
Total		22	100%	140	100%

In the above table 72.7% leaders and 41.4% members express that members are capable of discovering spiritual truths on their own and 27.3% leaders and 48.6% members believe that believers discover spiritual truths to some extent on their own. It is the aim of Christian education to impart the Christian values in a believer through which he/she can discover spiritual truths on their own.

Table 48. Do you seek curriculum that is relevant to the lives of the members?

Sl. No.	Options	Leaders		Members	
		Respondents	Percentage	Respondents	Percentage
a	Yes	12	54.5%	57	40.7%
b	Sometimes	10	45.5%	57	40.7%
c	No	-	-	6	4.2%
d	Not sure	-	-	20	14.4%
Total		22	100%	140	100%

According to table 48, 54.5% of leaders and 40.7% of members pursue a curriculum for Christian education that is relevant to the lives of the church members, whereas 45.5% leaders and 40.7% of members do it on rare occasions. Curriculum is a main constituent through which Christian education is imparted, which should be constructed on the foundations of theology, philosophy, sociology, and psychology.

Table 49. Obedience to the Word of God is a sign of spiritual maturity

Sl. No.	Options	Leaders		Members	
		Respondents	Percentage	Respondents	Percentage
a	Yes	20	90.9%	122	87.2%
b	To some extent	-	-	14	10%
c	No	2	9.1%	2	1.4%
d	Not sure	-	-	2	1.4%
Total		22	100%	140	100%

90.9% of the leaders and 87.2% of members agree that obedience to the Word of God is a sign of spiritual maturity as indicated in table 49. One's spiritual maturity can be analysed based on the lifestyle of the person and his/her obedience to the Word of God.

Table 50. A spiritual matured person is committed to God

Sl.No.	Options	P/L Respondents	Percentage
a	Yes	20	90.9%
b	To some extent	2	9.1%
c	No	-	-
d	May be	-	-
Total		22	100%

As shown in analysis of table 50, 90.9% of respondents agree that a spiritually matured person who is committed to God will grow spiritually, study the scriptures, and pray regularly. On the other hand, only 9.1% of them have complied that spiritual growth takes place with some extent.

Table 51. In the process of spiritual growth one develops love, patience, etc.

Sl. No.	Options	Leaders		Members	
		Respondents	Percentage	Respondents	Percentage
a	For sure	20	90.9%	124	88.6%
b	Sometimes	2	9.1%	10	7.1%
c	Not necessarily	-	-	2	1.4%
d	Not sure	-	-	4	2.9%
Total		22	100%	140	100%

In continuation to table 50 the above table (51) also discusses about the process of spiritual growth regarding being more compassionate, loving, patient, understanding, caring, forgiving, etc., to which 90.9% of leaders and 88.6% of members have agreed to the process of spiritual growth.

Table 52. Spiritual transformation is transforming into the image of Christ

Sl.No.	Options	P/L Respondents	Percentage
a	Yes	22	100.0%
b	To some extent	-	-
c	No	-	-
d	May be	-	-
Total		22	100%

According to table 52, 100% of the respondents agree that spiritual transformation is the process of nurturing a person to have an intimate relationship with God thereby transforming into the image of Christ.

Table 53. Spiritual formation leads to socialization with the community around

Sl. No	Options	Leaders		Members	
		Respondents	Percentage	Respondent	Percentage
a	Completely believe	18	81.8%	90	64.1%
b	To some extent	4	18.2%	38	26.1%
c	Do not believe	-	-	6	4.9%
d	I don't know	-	-	6	4.9%
Total		22	100%	140	100%

Based on the analysis in table 53, 81.8% leaders and 64.1% members completely believe spiritual formation also leads a person to have a better social life outside the church.

6. Holistic Transformation

Table 54. Christian education leads to holistic transformation of the churches

Sl. No.	Options	Leaders		Members	
		Respondents	Percentage	Respondents	Percentage
a	To great extent	20	90.9%	95	67.2%
b	To some extent	2	9.1%	35	25%
c	No	-	-	4	2.9%
d	Not sure	-	-	6	4.9%
Total		22	100%	140	100%

According to table 54, 90.9% of the leaders and 67.2% of members agree to a great extent that the main aim of Christian education should be leading the congregations towards holistic transformation.

Table 55. Do you impart Christian education in an acceptable method?

Sl.No.	Options	P/L Respondents	Percentage
a	Yes	22	100.0%
b	Sometimes	-	-
c	No	-	-
d	May be	-	-
Total		22	100%

According to table 59, 100% of respondents agree that adequate methods of imparting Christian education is practiced that will surely bring holistic transformation among congregations.

Table 56. Christian education happens in church contexts, thus, it is spiritual

Sl.No.	Options	P/L Respondents	Percentage
a	Yes	6	27.3%
b	Not necessarily	16	72.7%
c	No	-	-
d	Not sure	-	-
Total		22	100%

72.7% of respondents agree that Christian education is imparted not only in Sunday school settings but also out of church contexts according to the analysis shown in table 56.

Table 57. Members pursue alternatives for holistic development

Sl.No.	Options	P/L Respondents	Percentage
a	Many of them	4	18.2%
b	Few of them	12	54.5%
c	No	4	18.2%
d	No idea	2	9.1%
Total		22	100%

The above table discusses that members of the church are looking at alternatives for holistic development rather than Christian education. 54.5% agree that a few of them are looking for alternatives, 18.2% assume many members are anticipating for alternatives. In brief there are ample number of people turning towards other alternatives for holistic development.

Table 58. Are there any external barriers for holistic transformation?

Sl. No.	Options	Leaders		Members	
		Respondents	Percentage	Respondents	Percentage
a	Yes	16	72.7%	71	50.8%
b	Very few	2	9.1%	37	26.4%
c	No	2	9.1%	16	11.4%
d	May be	2	9.1%	16	11.4%
Total		22	100%	140	100%

There are external barriers for the members to experience holistic transformation like negative attitude towards Christian education, contextual issues in the church, etc., according to table 58, and 72.7% of leaders and 50.8% of members agree to this view.

Table 59. Is holistic transformation appreciated by members?

Sl. No.	Options	P/L Respondents	Percentage
a	Yes	16	72.7%
b	May Be	6	27.3%
c	No	-	-
Total		22	100%

Based on the analysis from table 59, 72.7% of the respondents agree that majority church members appreciate the holistic transformation and 27.3% expressed that only a few of them in the church are interested in holistic transformation. This proves that a good number of respondents do not nullify holistic development in a church context.

Table 60. Holistic transformation is possible through Christian education

Sl. No.	Options	P/L Respondents	Percentage
a	To great extent	18	81.8%
b	To some extent	4	18.2%
c	Not possible	-	-
d	No idea	-	-
Total		22	100%

In this final table from the leaders' questionnaire section, the leaders were asked whether the holistic transformation is possible through Christian education, which is approved by 81.8% of the respondents. Hence, it shows that the members are assured of holistic transformation in and through Christian education.

C. Members Questionnaire Analysis and Interpretation

1. Members' views on Christian Education

Table 61. Christian education is Biblically based ministry

Sl.No.	Options	Respondents	Percentage
a	Nowhere it is mentioned in the Bible	17	12.1%
b	Bible is the basis for Christian education	117	83.6%
c	It was included as ministry in the later stages of history	2	1.4%
d	Others	4	2.9%
Total		140	100%

With the above table members' questionnaire is introduced, and this table 83.6% of respondents agree that the Bible is the primary content of Christian education. Most of the respondents are aware that Christian education has its roots in the biblical times and probably this conviction led them to believe the Bible as the foundation for Christian education.

Table 62. In your opinion, the aim of Christian education in your church is

Sl. No.	Options	Respondents	Percentage
a	Intellectual/Cognitive Transformation	15	10.7%
b	Spiritual/Psychological Transformation	37	26.4%
c	Socio-Political Transformation	4	2.9%
d	All Inclusive	84	60%
Total		140	100%

According to table 62, aim of Christian education is all inclusive or the holistic transformation is what 60% of respondents agree. All inclusive or holistic means spiritual, intellectual, social and moral transformations. 40% respondents do not accept that Christian education strives towards the holistic transformation, this might be because they understand Christian education as spiritual and will help sometimes in intellectual or psychological development.

Table 63. These various transformations possible through Christian education?

Sl.No.	Options	Respondents	Percentage
a	To great extent	70	50%
b	To some extent	54	38.6%
c	No	4	2.9%
d	No Idea	12	8.5%
Total		140	100%

In continuation of table 62, this table also discusses about the various transformations and its possibilities through Christian education to which 50% agree to a great extent, and 38.6% agree to some extent. As mentioned earlier members are limited to spiritual and cognitive development through Christian education and there is a need to enlighten them that Christian education is capable of bringing holistic transformation and not limited to just one or few transformations.

Table 64. Is your pastor in consistence with aims of Christian education?

Sl.No.	Options	Respondents	Percentage
a	Yes	100	71.3%
b	Sometimes	26	18.6%
c	No	12	8.6%
d	No Idea	2	1.4%
Total		140	100%

The analysis in table 64 depict the consistency of the pastor's ministry in relation to Christian education's aim and objectives. The majority of the respondents that is 71.3% of them agree that impartation of Christian education is in accordance with the aims and objectives. There is a consistency in ministry of leaders regarding the aims and objectives of Christian education. However, there are some ambiguities where the ministry of Christian education in the church has to be considered.

Table 65. Holistic transformation is top priority in the church you attend

Sl.No.	Options	Respondents	Percentage
a	Yes	100	71.3%
b	Sometimes	24	17.1%
c	Never	8	5.7%
d	No idea	8	5.7%
Total		140	100%

According to table 65, 71.3% of the members agree that holistic transformation of all members is the top priority in the church they attend, 17.1% of members believe that sometimes the church prioritizes holistic transformation. It is also to be noted that about 30% claim that holistic transformation is not the top priority of the churches.

Table 66. Do you accept a pastor should be transformed spiritually first?

Sl.No.	Options	Respondents	Percentage
a	Yes	122	87.2%
b	To some extent	8	5.7%
c	No	2	1.4%
d	No idea	8	5.7%
Total		140	100%

According to table 66, 87.2% of the respondents agree that the pastor or teacher should be transformed to transform others. It is an important need for the church to have spiritually transformed leaders or teachers who will in turn make an effect in transforming other members.

Table 67. Christian education is supportive in developing intellectual capabilities

Sl.No.	Options	Respondents	Percentage
a	Certainly	110	78.6%
b	Doubtful	2	1.4%
c	May be	24	17.1%
d	No Idea	4	2.9%
Total		140	100%

According to the result shown in table 67, 78.6% of respondents favour that Christian education supports the development of intellectual capabilities. Thus, it is to be noted that Christian education has a dynamic role to play in the development of the intellectual abilities of the members in the church.

Table 68. Christian education brings awareness in social and cultural areas

Sl.No.	Options	Respondents	Percentage
a	Surely	120	85.7%
b	Sometimes	8	5.1%
c	No	2	1.4%
d	May be	6	4.9%
e	Any other	4	2.9%
Total		140	100%

The majority of the respondents that is 85.7% according to the table 68 agree that Christian education brings an awareness in social and cultural aspects. This result provides the information that social and cultural understandings are vital in the church context.

2. Cognitive or Intellectual Transformation

Table 69. Members are capable of defending their faith and practices

Sl.No.	Options	Respondents	Percentage
a	Yes	70	50.0%
b	To some extent	53	37.8%
c	No	5	3.6%
d	Not sure	12	8.6%
Total		140	100%

50% of respondents in the above table agree that the members of the church are capable of defending their faith and practices intellectually. 37.8% respondents agree to it to some extent. Thus, the table reveals the need for intellectual development among the believers, which is vital in the Christian educational Praxis.

3. Psychological Transformation

Table 70. Your pastor/teacher knows the basics of psychology

Sl.No.	Options	Respondents	Percentage
a	To great extent	82	58.8%
b	No	12	8.6%
c	Can't say	46	32.6%
Total		140	100%

58.6% of the members agree to great extent that their pastors or leaders are aware of the basic knowledge of psychology and the ministry is done accordingly as per table 70. Even though many agree that leaders have the knowledge of basics in psychology, the others disagree or not sure about it. This suggests that the need of the leaders' basic knowledge of psychology is important, without which the ministry be incompetent.

Table 71. Psychology could provide practical techniques

Sl.No.	Options	Respondents	Percentage
a	Most of the times	74	51.6%
b	Very rare	20	14.9%
c	Do not provide any help	6	4.9%
d	May be	40	28.6%
Total		140	100%

The above table state that 51.6% of them agree that most of the time basic understanding of psychology will provide practical techniques for Christian education, but 28.6% of them opine that it may help on rare occasions.

4. Socio–Cultural Transformation

Table 72. Is cultural transformation the work of individuals?

Sl.No.	Options	Respondents	Percentage
a	Yes	100	71.3%
b	To some extent	24	17.1%
c	No	8	5.8%
d	May be	8	5.8%
Total		140	100%

According to table 72, 71.3% of the respondents agree to great extent cultural transformation is the responsibility of an individual and not just the local church, and 17.1% of members agree it to some extent.

Table 73. Are the social relationships of the members developed?

Sl.No.	Options	Respondents	Percentage
a	Completely	80	57.1%
b	Based on the context	50	35.1%
c	That is not important	4	2.9%
d	Don't know	6	4.9%
Total		140	100%

Social relationships of members with the people in the community can be developed through Christian education, which is completely accepted by 57.1% members, whereas 35.1% members confine stating it is based on the context according to table 73. Christian education is certainly a main aspect through which social relationships can be improved.

Table 74. Christian education attempts to bring change in political views

Sl.No.	Options	Respondents	Percentage
a	To great extent	90	64.1%
b	To some extent	38	26.1%
c	No	6	4.9%
d	Not sure	6	4.9%
Total		140	100%

64.1% of respondents believe to great that Christian education plays a major role in bringing changes or attempts to bring change in the attitude of people's political views according to the analysis from table 74. Therefore, Christian education certainly brings changes in political views of the members either directly or indirectly.

5. Spiritual Transformation

Table 75. A spiritually matured person is committed to God

Sl.No.	Options	Respondents	Percentage
a	To great extent	110	78.6%
b	To some extent	24	17.1%
c	No	4	2.9%
d	May be	2	1.4%
Total		140	100%

The above table inquires about the opinion of the members whether a spiritually matured person will be committed to God and continually grows spiritually, reads the scriptures and prays regularly to which 78.6% of them agree it to a great extent, 17.1% agree to some extent, 2.9% disagree it, and the rest were not sure about it.

Table 76. Does spiritual transformation nurtures a person towards God?

Sl.No.	Options	Respondents	Percentage
a	Yes	120	85.8%
b	To some extent	12	8.4%
c	No	4	2.9%
d	May be	4	2.9%
Total		140	100%

The analysis of the table 76 shows that 85.8% of members responding positively that spiritual transformation is the process which nurtures a person to have an intimate relationship with God and transforms him/her into the image of Christ.

6. Holistic Transformation

Table 77. Does your pastor impart Christian education in an acceptable method?

Sl.No.	Options	Respondents	Percentage
a	To great extent	110	78.6%
b	To some extent	18	12.7%
c	No	4	2.9%
d	May be	8	5.8%
Total		140	100%

According to the table 77, majority of respondents that is 78.6% agree to a great extent that their pastor in the church is practicing an acceptable method in imparting Christian education in order to bring holistic transformation. If correct methods are adopted to impart Christian education, the target of holistic transformation may be possible.

Table 78. Christian education happens in the church contexts thus it is spiritual?

Sl.No.	Options	Respondents	Percentage
a	Yes	100	71.2%
b	To some extent	26	18.1%
c	No	6	4.9%
d	Not sure	8	5.8%
Total		140	100%

Based on the analysis of table 78, the majority members that is 71.2% believe Christian education takes place in church contexts like Sunday school therefore it is a spiritual matter only. Thus, we understand that the members still believe that Christian education is spiritual matter only, because it is practiced in church contexts.

Table 79. Church members look at alternatives for holistic development

Sl.No.	Options	Respondents	Percentage
a	Many of them	30	21.4%
b	Few of them	78	55.7%
c	None	14	10%
d	No idea	18	12.9%
Total		140	100%

According to table 79 which discusses about the members looking for alternatives than Christian education for holistic development received a mixed response. 55.7% respondents agree that few of them are indeed looking for alternatives. 21.4% assert many of the members are in search for alternatives. This table reveals that majority of people are looking for other alternatives for holistic development, which has to be taken on a serious note and make necessary amendments in the Praxis of Christian education to make it more appropriate for holistic development.

Table 80. Do you appreciate holistic transformation?

Sl.No.	Options	Respondents	Percentage
a	Yes	110	78.9%
b	Only sometimes	22	15.3%
c	No	4	2.9%
d	Not sure	4	2.9%
	Total	140	100%

The majority of members in table 80 that is 78.9% of them appreciate the holistic transformation, and 15.3% have limited to sometimes. Overall, the majority of them are looking forward to be transformed completely. Christian education is one of those main practices that can be used for the holistic transformation of the members or any common man.

Table 81. Holistic transformation is possible through Christian education

Sl.No.	Options	Respondents	Percentage
a	To great extent	97	69.2%
b	To some extent	33	23.7%
c	Not possible	4	2.9%
d	No idea	6	4.2%
	Total	140	100%

In conclusion, according to table 81 majority of members that is 69.2% agree that holistic transformation is possible through Christian education. Hence, many believe that Christian education is the primary source that can bring holistic transformation if it is imparted in a systematic manner taking into consideration the social, moral, spiritual, psychological, and intellectual aspects of the members.

Chapter 4

Research Findings, Suggestions, and Recommendations

Introduction

In this chapter, the researcher would like to bring out some major findings emerging out of the analysis of data specified in the previous chapter. Based on the findings, some suggestions are being made in regard to Christian Education toward the holistic transformation of congregations of the Southern Methodist Churches in India, with recommendations that are to be taken in to consideration for effective Christian Education.

A. Validity of the Hypothesis

On the whole a mixed result was found with regard to the hypothesis with this study assumed. It would not be fair to say that the SMCI is not aware of the needs of Christian education as far as it is generally understood. Yet as far as active involvement is concerned definitely the church is lethargic in the praxis of holistic approach to Christian education. Therefore, the hypothesis is justified to the great extent, that the SMCI leadership and members are little relaxed in relation to Holistic Transformation through Christian education. In other words, they lack a creative spirit and are incapable of improving the praxis of holistic approach to Christian Education.

B. Findings

1. Important Findings from Leaders

- Majority of the leaders have a positive opinion towards Christian education and feel it plays an important role in the process of spiritual transformation of an individual, church, and community.
- Majority of the leaders have confined that Christian education is something related to spiritual or faith formation. Social, cognitive, psychological transformations are less important to the leaders.
- The leaders understand that Christian education does not help in developing intellectual/cognitive capabilities, there is no need of intellectual believers, and does not believe in the need of participating in any scholarly teachings or lectures. Thus, the finding also provides information that not many members in the churches neither have a capacity of defending their faith and practice intellectually nor strive to develop their intellect.
- Majority of the leaders use similar methods in their educational activity irrespective of the age group of the learner. Thus, it is noted that the developmental stages are not considered as important or the leaders have no idea about it.
- The role of psychology in the ministry of leaders seem to be very inadequate, and important psychological theories that help Christian education are not used properly for the enrichment of educational ministry. This proves that leaders of SMCI do not adopt these theories for the impartation of Christian education.
- The members psychological development is something least aspect of ministry of the leaders of SMCI, thus, it is understood that psychological transformation is not given any importance by SMCI leaders.
- Socio-cultural transformation of members, the majority of the respondent leaders have little or no regard for this aspect.

- Social relationships of the members with community outside the church is not is not regarded by the leaders, this provides evidence that impartation of Christian education is not done towards developing social relationships.
- The present Christian education ministry of SMCI is limited to Faith or spiritual development, this understanding of the leaders shows that other transformations are not given importance in SMCI educational ministry.
- Rapport with the community around the church is ambiguous, which has to be addressed by the Christian educators with utmost importance.
- Indian political understanding of the people in the church is also not systematized, the political awareness is not transported by the church or the leaders to full extent.
- Despite Christian Education being holistic in nature and transformative, majority of the leaders have opined that Christian education is limited to faith or spiritual transformation.
- Majority of leaders accept that most of the members are looking towards other alternatives for holistic transformation, rather than Christian education itself.
- Above findings prove that SMCI and its Christian educational ministry is not effective in bringing holistic transformation but is concerned with only spiritual or faith related transformations.
- Thus, the findings from the leaders clarify that the Christian education in the SMCI is concentrating mainly on the spiritual transformation. SMCI leadership does not give any vitality to the Socio-Cultural, Psychological, and Cognitive transformation or development of the members within the churches. There should be an awakening among the leaders about the importance of holistic transformation in the congregations for which various activities towards that end has to be introduced and implemented in SMCI.

2. Important Findings from Members

- Although majority have accepted that holistic transformation is possible through Christian education, when inquired about the specific transformations like cognitive, psychological, and socio-cultural transformations they have expressed their reservations.

- Most of the members have rejected the idea of the need of intellectual believers in the church, who are analytical and logical, and there are also to a great number who do not give any importance to scholarly seminars or lectures which supports the intellect of the people.
- Reasonably a number of member respondents claimed that they very rarely or completely do not read any book/materials apart from Bible for their all-round development. This proves that the churches do not have proper resources or any printed material available for members and they are not encouraged by the pastors or leaders to do so, thus, the members are limited to Bible alone.
- It is also noted through the data, that many members do not try or strive to develop their intellectual capabilities. Christian education has a major role in helping the members for cognitive development.
- The other major finding is that the teaching or the preaching ministry of the leaders in SMCI is not helping members to develop intellectually or cognitively.
- Majority of members do not accept that psychology would help to understand human mental condition and in turn be a channel for essential faith formation. They also claim that their leaders do not adopt any psychological theories in imparting Christian education.
- Many of the members also do not accept that Bible contains many issues or answers related to psychological transformation, thus, it is understood that members look at Bible as only a faith transformer and not a holistic transformer.
- Majority members do not give regard to the socio-cultural awareness among the churches, and also opine that socio-cultural view cannot be transformed completely through Christian education.
- Christian education according to majority members do not help in social relationships, thus, it is to be noted that members have expressed their reservations in relation to development of sound

social relationships with people outside the church through Christian education.

- Cultural values are not imparted among the SMCI congregations in the praxis of Christian education according to the findings from the members.
- Majority of the members have accepted that spiritual transformation is possible through Christian education, but at the same time many contend that spiritual transformation does lead to socialization with the community around.
- Members are not in a solid position to discover spiritual truth unless the leader imparts to them, this proves that members are not developing in the spiritual maturity.
- Members believe that holistic transformation through Christian education is obvious, but they understand that there are external barriers that hinder the process, like socio-political situation of the area, economic destabilization in the society, contextual issues, negative attitude towards Christian education, etc., are few of them to mention.
- The findings clearly gives us a picture of how the people foresee Christian education and its implications. Bearing these in mind the researcher understands that members and as well the leaders are with an opinion of Christian education being a spiritual matter. Thus, the researcher has few suggestions which could be implemented in the SMCI congregations and apply the holistic approach to Christian education toward the complete transformation of the congregations.

C. Suggestions

Based on the findings of the empirical study, the researcher would like to make few recommendations for the improvement in praxis of Christian education towards holistic transformation of congregations of the SMCI. Few suggestions from the respondents were also incorporated in this section which will be followed by recommendations for effective Christian education.

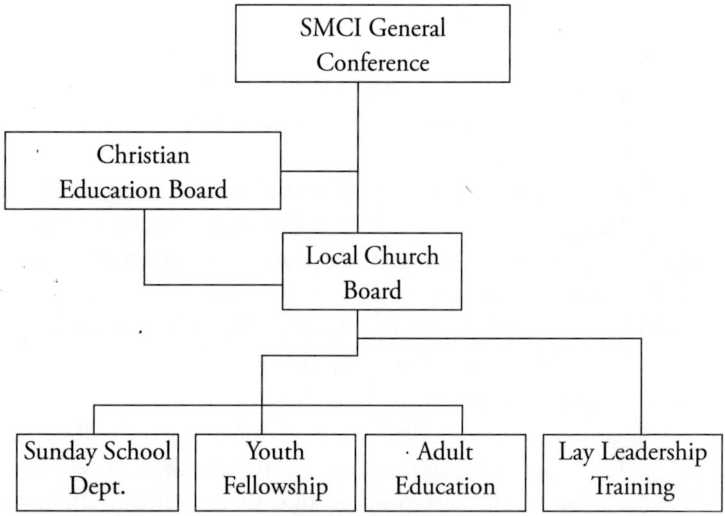

Figure 1: Chart of the Organization of Christian Education Board of SMCI

1. Organization of the Christian Education Board in SMCI

The SMCI has to develop Christian education department to improve and supervise the Christian education work in the General Conference level, but it has no proper management or structure at present. Decentralization of the departments is vital at this stage of growth in the church. The researcher proposes to establish Christian Education Board in the denomination and let other agencies of the local church like, Sunday school department, Youth Fellowship, Adult Education, Lay Leadership Training will be as functional agencies. Each local church with all the mentioned agencies will work under the leadership of the Board appointed by the General Conference of SMCI.

2. Importance of Christian Education in SMCI

The role of Christian education is to enable learner in church to grow spiritually, intellectually, physically and socially.[181] To be a

[181] Bernard Gechiko Nyabwari, Michael T Katola, and Daniel Muindi, "Holistic Christian Education for Character Formation in Seventh-Day Adventist Church Sponsored Secondary Schools in Nyamira County, Kenya," *International*

responsible citizen of society, a person must understand the world around him/her and recognize what it needs. In this way, Christian education helps learners to be able to discern what is good and evil by imparting wisdom which offers learners the ability to communicate and understand each other despite their social, religious, cultural and intellectual diversities.

Veith G. discuses about few principles learners require to make worthwhile decisions: creation of enabling environment, accommodation of other people's opinions, respect for other people's choices, following authorized procedures, doing interactive interrogation and consultation, facilitating group planning, maintaining support and being willing to take initiatives.[182] The task of SMCI pastors or leaders is to invite learners to imagine the consequences of Christian educational praxis and envision how an aspect of it can or should be reshaped to promote the well-being of others.

3. Objectives

The highest function of education is to bring about an integrated individual who is capable of dealing with life as a whole – J. Krishna Murthi.[183] Thus, the purpose of holistic Christian education in SMCI is to prepare members to meet the challenges of living as well as spirituality. Holistic Christian education believes it is important for people to learn: about themselves, about healthy relationships and pro-social behaviour, spiritual enhancement, emotional or psychological development, resilience, to experience transcendence, and appreciate some sense of truths, are thus, the main objectives of Christian education within SMCI.

Journal of Academic Research in Progressive Education and Development 2, no. 1 (January 2013): 248.

[182] G Veith, *"Dependable Treasure". A Lutheran Perspective on Vocation, Career, Preparation and Higher Education Today* (St. Loius: Concordia Seminary, 2006), 45.

[183] "Holistic Education: An Introduction, Page 3," *Holistic Education*, http:// www.holistic-education.net/visitors3.htm. Accessed January 23, 2017.

4. Teaching Methods

The empirical study analysis and interpretation brought forth various findings, and based on those findings the researcher has come to few conclusive understanding on the methods to impart Christian education for holistic transformation of SMCI congregations which can be traced in the following three points. The researcher has adopted Byron Anderson's three focal points on teaching methods like contemplative looking, contemplative reading, and contemplative play.[184]

a. Contemplative Looking

Reflective observation in other words contemplative looking, in its Latin form, means, "to observe, consider, or gaze attentively."[185] Reflection is first and foremost about "seeing." Seeing may be believing, but we must also believe in order to see. More, to see truly requires more than a passing glance which requires focused, contemplative looking. Christian education in SMCI shall enable the learner to have a reflective observation on the teaching imparted and this is the primary concern of the teaching method.

b. Contemplative Reading

As we think about contemplative reading, we realize that much of our reading, except perhaps our reading of fiction, is *informational* rather than *formational*.[186] Formational reading or sacred reading should be identified as the strong reading practice, which is more of seeking than about finding according to Michael Casey.[187] Helping the learners to seek the scriptures and interpret it accordingly, which would boost the holistic understanding of the learners of SMCI.

---

[184] E. Byron Anderson, "STOP, LOOK, LISTEN: CONTEMPLATIVE TEACHING AND LEARNING," *Christian Education Journal*, 3, 10, no. 2 (2013): 392–406.

[185] D Haynes, "Mindfulness and Contemplative Practice in Art and Religion," in *Meditation and the Classroom*, ed. J. Brown Simler and F Grace (New York: Suny Publishers, 2011), 223.

[186] R. Muholland, *Shaped by the Word* (Nashville: Upper Room, 1985), 47–60.

[187] Michael Casey, *Sacred Readings: The Ancient Art of Lectio Divina* (Ligouri: Ligouri, 1996), 8.

c. Contemplative Play

Jerome Berryman's understanding of play as a form of *knowledge of God* rather than as a device for *knowledge about God* bears some similarity to understanding of play, particularly as play, participation, and theoria (or contemplation).[188] This play requires a story, people to play together, space and time to play, and leaders/teachers involvement in it. It will be a learner-centred that helps the learners in SMCI to reflect in the play and comprehend the knowledge of God.

5. Content

Christian education in general is understood as a set of imparting biblical content, stories and creeds. It is used as a process of conditioning the mind, body and spirit of learners according to the popularly accepted norms and beliefs of the Church and society. But, Christian education is much more and very different from the above mentioned intention. As Herbert Hoeffer concisely remarked:

> The aim of Christian education is much more radical and dynamic. The emphasis is not knowing but becoming. Christian education is the process of relating God's people to the challenges and opportunities of their lives in His service.[189]

This means Christian education is a process in which the learner is facilitated to look at his or her faith in relation to scripture, traditions of the Church as well as to the Indian context and to the life situations. No doubt Christian heritage and tradition which includes the Bible, liturgical tradition and rituals help us to keep our identity. Particularly at the present time where media explosion has sneaked into the lives of our younger generation, they are losing their interest in the religious life of the Church as they feel the way Christian religious way of teaching is not on par with recent media techniques.

---

[188] Jerome Berryman, *Godly Play: A Way of Religious Education* (San Francisco: Harper & Row, 1991), 87–89.

[189] Herbert Hoeffer, ed., *Debate on Missions* (Madras: Gurukul Lutheran Theological College and Research, 1979), 448.

Karl Barth advised leaders to preach with the Bible in one hand and the newspaper in the other.[190] That is good advice for living as well. Live with the Bible, our confessions, our prayers, and the rest of our meaningful traditions in one hand while holding the world around us in the other. Within the SMCI's Christian education, Bible shall not be the only content, but context also.

6. Social and Cultural Awareness

For the learner's personal and social development, the Christian educators of SMCI should aim to:

Teach Biblical views for personal and social relationships. (Psalms. 119:9; Luke 10:27; 1 Thessalonians. 4:6). Teach the learners to treat their neighbour with love and respect as unique individuals created in God's image (Matthew. 5:44; John 14:21; 1 Corinthians. 13:4, 5; 1 John 3:18; Ephesians. 5:21). Teach a Biblical view of marriage, family, and community. (1 Thessalonians. 4:7; 1 Timothy. 4:12; Genesis. 2:18-25; Ephesians. 5:22- 33; Hebrews. 13:4). Promote physical fitness, good health habits, and wise use of the body as the temple of God. (1 Corinthians. 6:19). Emphasize the privileges and responsibilities of citizenship and an appreciation for the heritage or culture of freedom which we enjoy in India. (1 Corinthians. 10:11; Romans. 13:1-7; 1 Timothy. 2:1, 2). Based on these scriptures, social and cultural awareness programmes are to be organized for the members of SMCI on regular intervals.

7. Scholarly Seminars

These scholarly seminars and trainings will enable the church members to carry out the great commission locally and globally, develop the cognitive or analytical capabilities, increase the spiritual aptitude, helps the learner to be rational in many aspects of spirituality, and will not fall prey to the wrong teachings in the present context. Thus, the researcher perceives that SMCI should hold scholarly seminars on regular occasions which will produce many intellectual believers who will be an added asset to the church for the future ministry.

---

190 Hannibal Cabral, "Mission in the Context of Plurality," *World Council of Churches* (blog), accessed June 13, 2016, http://wcc-coe.org/wcc/what/interreligious/cd32-05.html. Accessed June 13, 2016.

8. Leadership Training

The busyness of a vibrant church gives little time for Christian leaders to focus on self-improvement. While thriving in their pastoral duties, ministry leaders can easily ignore the deficient areas of their lives.[191] These Christian leaders need an opportunity to reflect on life and ministry, clarifying hopes and dreams, as well as personal issues that hold them back. Once these leaders are equipped and updated they will be transformative channels in the congregations. At present there is no proper administration and curriculum for this training program. The researcher proposes for a planned training for the leaders of SMCI with the following curriculum outline for one year:

First Quarter: Foundational Courses

1. Introduction to the Old and New Testaments
2. Basic Doctrines
3. Christian Experience and Witness
4. Teaching Methods

Second Quarter:

1. Introduction to Christian Education
2. Inductive Study of the Scripture
3. History of Israel
4. Basics in Psychology and Sociology

Third Quarter:

1. Christian Education among Children, Youth, and Adults
2. Interpretation of Scriptures
3. Understanding Society
4. Leadership and Personality Skills

D. Recommendations for Effective Christian Education

In this section the situation of Christian education as described so far, some measures have to be put in place to correct the status quo

[191] Gregory B. Baxter, "A Leadership Training Material for the 21st Century Church Leader Based on the Pattern and Principles Jesus Created to Train the Twelve Apostles," *Journal of Applied Christian Leadership* 5, no. 2 (2011): 116.

in Christian education in the SMCI to the extent that it is humanly possible to bring holistic transformation. Thus, the aim is to come up with recommendations for effective Christian education for the SMCI and make the holistic transformation of the congregations possible.

1. The Advancement of Christian Education in Churches

The Christian Church is commissioned to teach, but its pastors are not always committed to the teaching ministry. Jesus in His missionary mandate commanded His disciples to go forth making disciples of all nations baptizing and *teaching* them (Mathew 28:16-20). Paul writes to Timothy and admonished him to entrust the Gospel to faithful men who were "apt to teach" (II Timothy 2:24), he is to teach the "Holy Scriptures" (II Timothy 3:14-17). The Apostolic church was a teaching church (Acts 5:42).

One of the recommendations (perhaps the first) for effective Christian education in future is that of engaging promotional activities with a view to conscientizing churches about the importance and the way of Christian education.[192] Such promotional activities have to be carried out at all levels of SMCI congregations.

2. Establishing Sound Administration

A machine, no matter how carefully built, will not function without power. So also human organizations whether they be political, social, or ecclesiastical must have personnel in order to be effective. A well-adjusted machine operates quietly; so does also a well-adjusted church administration related to Christian Education in this case.

The second major strategy that makes up for effective Christian education in future for SMCI is the embracing of a sound administration of Christian education in churches. Administration refers to 'the guidance, leadership, and control of the efforts of a group of individuals toward some common goal.'[193] Sound administration

---

[192] Matshiga, "Christian Education in the Baptist Convention of South Africa with Special Reference to Churches in the Transvaal: A Practical Theological Investigation," 261.

[193] T.O. Barnard and K.S. Rice, "Principles of Administration," in *Exploring Christian Education*, ed. A.E. Sanner and A.F. Harper (Kansas City: Beacon Hill

is comprised of various components. For Christian Education and the enhancement of its effectiveness, the following components of administration need consideration. They are, planning, the setting up of goals, putting a committee in place, adequate resources and facilities, organizing, budgeting, coordination or controlling of operations, and evaluation.[194] The purpose of sound administration is two-fold, first to facilitate the functioning of each unit; and second, to coordinate the different functional agencies.

3. Target Groups in Christian Education

The teaching is to extend to all ages as well as to all nations. The church is so accustomed to associating the term *children* with teaching, which is often forgotten that the teaching program of the church should include all ages "from cradle to the grave."

The effectiveness of Christian education in future also hinges upon the pride of place given to learners in the Church.[195] In any church setting, there are three basic levels of learners, namely, children, youth, and adults. Each category of learners need to be taught separately, as per their curriculum, capacity for comprehension, growth and understanding.

4. Curriculum Development

The traditional teaching materials have consisted of the *Bible History* and *Catechism.* The former has been a paraphrase of the historical events as recorded in the Bible with supplementary bridge between the two testaments. The catechism is a doctrinal study consisting of questions, answers, and supporting Bible passages.

Curriculum development can be used as another strategy for effective Christian education in the SMCI, though it may be regarded in other quarters as a routine imperative. The state of affairs in Christian education is such that the designing of a good

---

Press, 1978), 375.

[194] Matshiga, "Christian Education in the Baptist Convention of South Africa with Special Reference to Churches in the Transvaal: A Practical Theological Investigation," 268.

[195] R. Hestenes, H. Hendricks, and E. Palmer, *Mastering Teaching* (Portland: Christianity Today, 1991), 89.

curriculum for Christian education in many churches can serve as another factor for bringing about effective church educational ministry.[196] The designing of a curriculum is bound to bring about orderliness and direction in a given Christian education programme, hence the researcher refer to it as being another strategy for high quality Christian education, along with all other recommendations mentioned so far.

5. The Process of Christian Education

Along with all other recommendations discussed so far, is the component of process. Process has to do with how teaching unfolds. It refers to everything involved to make learning possible; the dynamics by which learning and teaching experience happens.[197] In other words, it has to do with the how of teaching and learning. Process includes among others the teacher, the learner, and the method of teaching. This process has been referred to in some way under 'Learners in Christian education' especially as it related to developmental stages in learners.

Modern methods of teaching may be used even when using traditional lesson materials. There may be class discussion, projections, occasional written and oral quizzes, modern technology or digital lesson plans, etc.

6. The Recruitment and Training of Leaders

The recruitment and training of leaders for Christian education is one of the major recommendations in the enhancing of effective Christian education in SMCI. It is generally agreed that the recruitment and training of leadership for the church educational ministry is very important. It cannot be replaced by any other component of ministry

---

[196] C.O. Galloway, "Principles of Curriculum Development," in *Exploring Christian Education*, ed. A.E. Sanner and A.F. Harper (Kansas City: Beacon Hill Press, 1978), 162.

[197] David S. Schuller, "The Local Church as Teacher: A Portrait," in *Rethinking Christian Education: Explorations in Theory and Practice*, ed. David S. Schuller (St. Loius: Chalice Press, 1993), 3.

whatsoever.[198] The Bible supports the recruitment and training of leadership. Further, the leadership thus adopted must fulfil certain conditions. Such leadership should, however, be equipped – with skills, knowledge, teaching ability, etc., for the educational ministry of the church.

For all practical purposes the pastor is the leadership recruiting officer for the church as well as for the denomination. The pastor of a small charge has a decided advantage in this respect than the pastor of a larger congregation. It is not enough that the church recruits leaders, the church is responsible for training them as well.

7. Effective Discipleship Programme

The implementation of an effective discipleship programme in SMCI is another important milestone en route to an effective Christian education programme. A discipleship programme is the starting point for all Christians and leaders.[199] No single leader can be effective in his leadership if he/she has not been properly discipled. In the final analysis all Christian education programmes must begin with discipleship. This is where the Christian journey begins. Jesus also began His journey with the disciples at this point, before He could entrust them with the task of making disciples of all nations.

The discipling process of Jesus was underscored by some factors. First, He called the 12, saying He would make them fishers of people (Mark 1: 17). Clearly, His mission was to prepare them for ministry in later years. During His stay with them He also called other people to repentance in their presence so they could see how He went about with His ministry. Secondly, He taught them God's Word; that is, what was to become the beginning of the New Testament, as recorded in the four gospels. In so doing He built them up and strengthened their faith. The apostles had their human problems though, but He did not give up on them; He continued to build them up and prayed for them so they could stand (John 17:9-20).

---

[198] Mark H. Senter, "Principles of Leadership Recruitment," in *Christian Education: Foundations for the Future*, ed. R.E. Clark, L. Johnson, and A.K. Sloat (Chicago: Moody Press, 1991), 469.

[199] J.T. Sisemore, *The Ministry of Religious Education* (Nashville: Broadman Press, 1978), 83.

8. Pastoral Involvement

As administrative head of the local church, pastor is responsible for all of the activities sponsored by the church. Even a small church, he will discover before long that if he tries to do it all himself, he will be spreading out his services so thin that his entire ministry becomes superficial.

Pastoral involvement in Christian education is very critical. In researcher's opinion it ranks first in importance among all other recommendations for effective Christian education in future. No Christian education will be effective without the blessing of the pastor.[200] If he does not support Christian education, it will not be easy to win the support of the church for the same. This makes pastoral involvement in Christian education an indispensable undertaking. Pastoral leadership is the key to the growth and success of church ministry in general and to Christian education in particular.

9. The Evaluation

In the last instance evaluation of Christian education, though a part of administration, is so important that like other aforementioned recommendations, it should be treated as a special aspect. In some of the instances where Christian education was done, lack of proper evaluation of the total programme might have partly led to poor performance or the ultimate collapse of the programme.[201] Many articles devoted to the evaluation of Christian education in many books testify to the importance of evaluation for the success of Christian education in churches. Thus, the SMCI leadership should give a special interest to the evaluation process.

Randolph Crump Miller concludes his stimulating book *Education for Christian Living* (1956) with these words, "With all of our plans and standards and techniques and theological insights, it is God who does the educating. We are channels of His grace doing the planting and watering, and the increase is a gift of God." It reflects

---

[200] Donald M. Geiger, "The Pastor's Educational Ministry," in *Christian Education: Foundations for the Future*, ed. R.E. Clark, L. Johnson, and A.K. Sloat (Chicago: Moody Press, 1991), 411.

[201] Hestenes, Hendricks, and Palmer, *Mastering Teaching*, 106.

as Paul writes in I Corinthians 3:6, "I have planted, Apollos watered, but God gave the increase." We are not responsible for the growth, the Spirit of God works in the hearts of humans, we are to sow, water, and cultivate.

Conclusion

In this chapter the researcher has outlined few major findings of the study, based on these findings, some suggestions and recommendations for effective Christian education that leads to holistic transformation of the congregations of SMCI are specified. There is a definite need to clearly define the objectives, develop the mode of imparting Christian education, bringing forth an effective curriculum, training the leaders in an amicable manner so that the congregations be transformed in all areas of life and be relevant in the present day context of India in general and Telangana & Andhra Pradesh in particular.

General Conclusion

Earlier on, the researcher indicated that several factors prompted the research into Christian education in the churches of the Southern Methodist Church in India. Among others, the holistic approach to Christian education in the Southern Methodist Churches, i.e., the way in which it was done, and the impact made by leaders and the members in their approach to Christian education. The aim of the research was to bring to light limitations and strengths in the educational ministry of the SMCI and thereupon prescribe remedial measures for the way forward.

In the first chapter, researcher has stated the problem at hand, namely that while SMCI is involved in Christian education in varying degrees, there is a great need to improve on what is being done or to start all over again for those who were not so involved. The researcher also explained the purpose of the research, in light of the problem already stated, and how the research would unfold.

The second chapter dwelt on the historical development of Christian education from the Old Testament times. The researcher has devoted attention to three areas mainly, the Old Testament, New Testament, and the meaning, purpose, concept of holistic Christian Education. The aim of this chapter was to give an overview of Christian education in the early years, so that whatever is taking place now in Christian education, is in large measure, the product of history.

In the third chapter researcher has outlined detailed empirical data with the interpretation of Holistic Christian Education in the SMCI, as well as describing the current situation in respect of Christian education in the same churches, based on the responses received through questionnaires from church leaders and members.

The data analysis process in the third chapter, led to chapter four, which was concerned with important findings, suggestions, and recommendations for effective Christian education for holistic transformation of the congregations in future for the SMCI as well as the Church of Jesus Christ in general.

The entire research exercise was interesting, challenging, worth a while, and yet not so easy an undertaking. Yet, the researcher wish that the suggestions and recommendations for effective Christian education for holistic transformation of congregations of SMCI become more adequate in its educational ministry.

In conclusion, the researcher pray and hope that the research discourse at hand will, those focused on (holistic) Christian Education and other church leaders, a genuine desire to reflect more on what is going on in the educational ministry of churches in India; to interact meaningfully with churches in this regard and to come up with new ways of enhancing effectiveness in Christian education.

Bibliography

Books

Astley, J. "Definitions, Aims and Approaches: An Overview." In *Critical Perspectives on Christian Education: A Reader on the Aims, Principles and Philosophy of Christian Education*, edited by J. Astley and L.F. Francis, 3–12. Herefordshire: Gracewing Fowler Wright Books, 1994.0.

———. *The Philosophy of Christian Religious Education*. Birmingham: Religious Education Press, 1994.

Barnard, T.O., and K.S. Rice. "Principles of Administration." In *Exploring Christian Education*, edited by A.E. Sanner and A.F. Harper, 366–85. Kansas City: Beacon Hill Press, 1978.

Berryman, Jerome. *Godly Play: A Way of Religious Education*. San Francisco: Harper & Row, 1991.

Berube, Darcy. *Religious Education at a Crossroads: Moving on in the Freedom of the Spirit*. New Jersey: Paulist Press, 1995.

Bharata. *The Natyashastra*. Translated by Manmohan Ghosh. Calcutta: Manisha Granthalaya, 1967.

Brueggemann, Walter. *Creative Word: Canon as a Model for Biblical Education*. Minneapolis: Fortress Press, 1982.

Burrow, Thomas. *Collected Papers on Dravidian Linguistics*. Madras: Annamalai University, 1968.

Casey, Michael. *Sacred Readings: The Ancient Art of Lectio Divina*. Ligouri: Ligouri, 1996.

Conder, Josiah. *The Modern Traveller: A Popular Description, Geographical, Historical, and Topographical of the Various Countries of the Globe*. Vol. 1. London: James Duncan, 1828.

Downs, Perry. "Promoting Moral Growth and Development." In *Street Children*. California: MARC, 1997.

———. *Teaching for Spiritual Growth*. Grand Rapids: Zondervan, 1994.

Eavey, C.B. *History of Christian Education*. Chicago: Moody Press, 1964.

Elkind, David. *The Child and Society: Essays in Applied Child Development*. New York: Oxford University Press, 1979.

Estep Jr., James R. "Moral Development and Christian Formation." In *Christian Formation: Integrating Theology & Human Development*, edited by James R. Estep Jr. and Jonathan H. Kim, 123–59. Nashville: B & H Academic, 2010.

Estep Jr., James R., Michael J. Anthony, and Gregg R. Allison. *A Theology for Christian Education*. Nashville: B & H Academic, 2008.

Forbes, Scot. "Values in Holistic Education." In *Education, Spirituality and the Whole Child*, 1–9. London: Roehampton Institute, 1996.

Fowler, James W. *Stages of Faith*. San Francisco: Harper & Row, 1981.

Frawley, William. *Vygotsky and Cognitive Science: Language and the Unification of the Social and Computational Mind*. Cambridge: Harvard University Press, 1997.

Galloway, C.O. "Principles of Curriculum Development." In *Exploring Christian Education*, edited by A.E. Sanner and A.F. Harper, 161–86. Kansas City: Beacon Hill Press, 1978.

Gangel, Kenneth O., and Warren S. Benson. *Christian Education: Its History and Philosophy*. Chicago: Moody Press, 1983.

Geiger, Donald M. "The Pastor's Educational Ministry." In *Christian Education: Foundations for the Future*, edited by R.E. Clark, L. Johnson, and A.K. Sloat. Chicago: Moody Press, 1991, 411-26.

Groome, Thomas. *Christian Religious Education: Sharing Our Story and Vision*. San Francisco: Harper & Row, 1980.

———. *Will there Be Faith? A New Vision for Educating and Growing Disciples*. New York: HarperOne, 2011.

Habermas, Ronald T. *Introduction to Christian Education and Formation: A Lifelong Plan for Christ-Centered Restoration*. Grand Rapids: Zondervan, 2008.

Harries, Jim. "Critiquing the Holistic Gospel." *Alliance for Vulnerable Mission Bulletin*, April 2013.

Haynes, D. "Mindfulness and Contemplative Practice in Art and Religion." In *Meditation and the Classroom*, edited by J. Brown Simler and F Grace, 223–28. New York: Suny Publishers, 2011.

Hestenes, R., H. Hendricks, and E. Palmer. *Mastering Teaching*. Portland: Christianity Today, 1991.

Hoeffer, Herbert, ed. *Debate on Missions*. Madras: Gurukul Lutheran Theological College and Research, 1979.

Kim, Jonathan H. "Intellectual Development and Christian Formation." In *Christian Formation: Integrating Theology & Human Development*, edited by James R. Estep Jr. and Jonathan H. Kim, 63–97. Nashville: B & H Academic, 2010.

Krathwohl, David R., Benjamin S. Bloom, and Bertram B. Masic. *Taxonomy of Educational Objectives: Handbook 2 - Affective Domain*. New York: Longmans, 1964.

Liddell, Henry George, and Robert Scott. *A Greek-English Lexicon*. Oxford: The Clarendon Press, 1968.

Maddix, Mark A. "Spiritual Formation and Christian Formation." In *Christian Formation: Integrating Theology & Human Development*, edited by James R. Estep Jr. and Jonathan H. Kim, 237–71. Nashville: B & H Academic, 2010.

Miller, John P. *Education and the Soul: Toward a Spiritual Curriculum*. New York: Suny Publishers, 2000.

Miller, Randolph Crump. *Education for Christian Living*. New Jersey: Prentice Hall, 1956.

Miller, Ron. *What Are Schools For? Holistic Education in American Culture*. 3rd Edition. Brandon, VT: Holistic Education Press, 1997.

Miranda, E.O. "Some Problems with the Expression 'Christian Education.'" In *Critical Perspectives on Christian Education: A Reader on the Aims, Principles and Philosophy of Christian Education*, edited by J. Astley and L.F. Francis, 16–23. Herefordshire: Gracewing Fowler Wright Books, 1994.

Mithra, H.G. "Christian Education: Agent of Liberation and Transformation." In *Becoming a Missional Congregation in the Twenty-First Century Indian Context*, edited by Jangkholam Haokip and Sungjemmeren K. Imchen, 118–34. Delhi: ISPCK, 2016.

———. *Wesley's Philosophy of Education for Socio-Spiritual Change*. New Delhi: Christian World Imprints, 2016.

Molholland, M. Robert. *Invitation to a Journey: A Road Map for Spiritual Formation*. Downers Grove: InterVarsity Press, 1993.

Moore, Mary Elizabeth. *Education for Continuity and Change*. Nashville: Abingdon Press, 1983.

Moran, G. "Of a Kind and to a Degree: A Roman Catholic Perspective." In *Does the Church Really Want Religious Education: An Ecumenical Inquiry*, edited by M. Myer, 15–31. Birmingham: Religious Education Press, 1988.

Muholland, R. *Shaped by the Word*. Nashville: Upper Room, 1985.

Myers, Bryant. *Walking with the Poor: Principles and Practices of Transformational Development*. Maryknoll: Orbis Books, 1998.

Neal, Cynthia J. "A Parenting Style for Nurturing Christian Wisdom." In *Limning the Psyche: Explorations in Christian Psychology*, edited by R. Roberts and M. Talbot, 165–85. Eugene, Oregon: Wipf and Stock, 2003.

Pazmino, Robert W. *Foundational Issues in Christian Education*. Second Edition. Grand Rapids: Baker Books, 1997.

———. *Foundational Issues in Christian Education: An Introduction in Evangelical Perspective*. First Edition. Grand Rapids: Baker Academic, 1988.

———. *Principles and Practices of Christian Education*. Grand Rapids: Baker Books, 1992.

Peters, R.S. *Essays on Educators*. London: Allen and Unwin, 1981.

Peterson, Eugene H. *Working with Angles*. Grand Rapids: William Eerdmans, 1987.

Piaget, Jean. *Genetic Epistemology*. New York: Columbia University Press, 1970.

———. *The Child and Reality: Problem of Genetic Psychology*. New York: Grossman, 1972.

———. *The Psychology of the Child*. New York: Basic Books, 1969.

Prabhakar, Samson. *Essay on Christian Education and Liturgy*. Bangalore: SATHRI, 2003.

Raths, Louis E., Merrill Harmin, and Sidney B. Simon. *Values and Teaching: Working with Values in the Classroom*. Columbus: Charles E Merrill Publishers, 1966.

Richards, Lawrence. *A Theology of Christian Education*. Grand Rapids: Zondervan, 1975.

Scharf, Peter. "Indoctrination, Values Clarification, and Developmental Moral Education as Educational Responses to Conflict and Change in Contemporary Society." In *Readings in Moral Education*, edited by Peter Scharf, 18–35. Minneapolis: Winston Press, 1978.

Schuller, David S. "The Local Church as Teacher: A Portrait." In *Rethinking Christian Education: Explorations in Theory and Practice*, edited by David S. Schuller, 3–15. St. Loius: Chalice Press, 1993.

Selvaraj, A. *Christianity and Social Transformation: A Kerala Story*. Trivandrum: ICRO, 2002.

Sema, Akheto. *Understanding the Nature and Purpose of Christian Religious Education*. Delhi: ISPCK, 2011.

Senter, Mark H. "Principles of Leadership Recruitment." In *Christian Education: Foundations for the Future*, edited by R.E. Clark, L. Johnson, and A.K. Sloat, 467–79. Chicago: Moody Press, 1991.

Siejk, Kate. "Toward a Holistic Religious Education: Reflections and Pedagogical Possibilities." In *Association of Professors and Researchers in Religious Education Conference*, 271–92. Fort Worth, Texas: Gonzaga University, 1993.

Sisemore, J.T. *The Ministry of Religious Education*. Nashville: Broadman Press, 1978.

Smith, Sherring. *History of Christianity in India*. Madras: Christian Literature Society, 1895.

Srihari, R. "Sanskrit and Telugu Literature." In *Proceedings of the Andhra Pradesh Oriental Conference: Fourth Session, Nagarjuna University, Guntur, 3rd to 5th March 1984*, 95–115. Michigan: University of Michigan, 1984.

Thanzauva, K. *Transforming Theology: A Theological Basis for Social Transformation*. Bangalore: Asian Trading Corporation, 2002.

Veith, G. *"Dependable Treasure." A Lutheran Perspective on Vocation, Career, Preparation and Higher Education Today*. St. Loius: Concordia Seminary, 2006.

Vygotsky, L.S. "On Psychological Systems." In *The Collected Works of L. S. Vygotsky: Problems of the Theory and History of Psychology*, edited by R.W. Rieber and J. Wollock, 3:91–108. New York: Plenum Press, 1930.

Wadley, Susan. *The Powers of Tamil Women*. Syracuse: Syracuse University Press, 1980.

Westerhoff, John H. *Tomorrow's Church: A Community of Change*. Waco, TX: Word Books, 1976.

Whitehead, A.N. *The Aims of Education and Other Essays*. New York: The Free Press, 1967.

Wilcox, M.M. *Developmental Journey*. Nashville: Abingdon Press, 1979.

Wilhoit, James C. *Spiritual Formation as if the Church Mattered*. Grand Rapids: Baker Books, 2008.

Wilken, Robert. *The Christians as the Romans Saw Them*. New Haven: Yale University Press, 1984.

Willard, Dallas. *The Great Omission: A Reclaiming; Jesus' Essential Teaching on Discipleship*. San Francisco: Harper Collins, 2006.

Wyckoff, Campbell D. *The Task of Christian Education*. Philadelphia: The Westminster Press, n.d.

Journals and Magazines

Anderson, E. Byron. "STOP, LOOK, LISTEN: CONTEMPLATIVE TEACHING AND LEARNING." *Christian Education Journal*, 3, 10, no. 2 (2013): 392–406.

Baxter, Gregory B. "A Leadership Training Material for the 21st Century Church Leader Based on the Pattern and Principles Jesus Created to Train the Twelve Apostles." *Journal of Applied Christian Leadership* 5, no. 2 (2011): 116–17.

Beck, Brenda. "The Symbolic Merger of Body, Space, and Cosmos in Hindu Tamil Nadu." *Contributions to Indian Sociology* 10, no. 2 (1976): 213–43.

Bragg, Wayne G. "Beyond Development to Transformation." *International Review of Mission* 73, no. 290 (April 1984): 153–65.

Cooper, Robert M. "Moral Formation in the Parish Church." *Anglican Theological Review* 69, no. 3 (1987): 268–85.

Kang, S. Steve, and Michael Feldman. "Transformed by the Transfiguration: Reflections on a Biblical Understanding of Transformation and Its Implications for Christian Education." *Christian Education Journal*, 3, 10, no. 2 (2013): 365–77.

Kumalo, Simanga R. "Southern African Sources for an Authentic Christian Education for Social Transformation." *Journal of Theology for Southern Africa* 122 (July 2005): 59–75.

Lim, David S. "Curriculum for Economic Transformation." *William Carey International Development Journal* 2, no. 4 (Fall 2013): 5–18.

Moyle, Helen. "The Experience of Learning." *The Way* 37, no. 2 (1997): 112–21.

Mulaa, Joseph Muyomi. "Life Skills Education: A Model for Socio-Cultural Transformation." *African Ecclesial Review* 54, no. 3&4 (2012): 305–35.

Nyabwari, Bernard Gechiko, Michael T Katola, and Daniel Muindi. "Holistic Christian Education for Character Formation in Seventh-Day Adventist Church Sponsored Secondary Schools in Nyamira County, Kenya." *International Journal of Academic*

Research in Progressive Education and Development 2, no. 1 (January 2013): 244–57.

Old, Hughes Oliphant. "What Is Reformed Spirituality? Played Over Again Lightly." *Calvin Studies* 7 (1994): 61–68.

Simundson, Daniel J. "Priest, Prophet, Wisdom Teacher: Old Testament Models of the Minister." *Word & World* IX, no. 4 (Fall 1989): 351–58.

Smallbones, Jackie L. "Teaching Bible for Transformation." *Christian Education Journal*, 3, 4, no. 2 (2007): 293–307.

Wallace, Thomas P. "Values and Spirituality: Enriching Curriculum Development and Teaching/Learning Processes for a New Millennium." *Journal of Christian Education* 43, no. 1 (May 2000): 41–49.

Wilkie, Au S.J. "Holistic Catechesis: Keeping Our Balance in the 1990s." *Religious Education* 86, no. 3 (Summer 1991): 347–60.

Dictionaries and Encyclopaedias

Aron, I, W Cutter, S.S. Lee, and M. Zeldon. "Jewish Education." Edited by Iris V. Cully and Kendig Brubaker Cully. *Harper's Encyclopedia of Religious Education*. New York: Harper & Row, 1990, 334-41.

Basista, Jakob. "India." Edited by George Thomas Kurian. *Encyclopaedia of the World's Nations and Cultures*. New Delhi: Viva Books, 2007, 1063-81.

Bercot, David W., ed. "Prophecy, Prophets." *A Dictionary of Early Christian Beliefs*. Massachusetts: Hendrickson Publishers, 1998, 538-41.

Bhushan, B., ed. "Social Change." *Anmol Dictionary of Sociology*. New Delhi: Anmol Publications, 1989, 285.

Buswell Jr, James Oliver. "Priest, Priesthood." Edited by Merrill C. Tenney and Steven Barabas. *The Zondervan Pictorial Bible Dictionary*. Grand Rapids: Zondervan, 1963, 682-83.

Eiselen, F.C. "Education in Old Testament Times." Edited by John T. McFarland and Benjamin S. Winchester. *The Encyclopaedia of Sunday Schools and Religious Education*. New York: Thomas Nelson & Sons, 1915, 363-68.

Ghiloni, Aaron J. "Holistic Christian Education." Edited by George Thomas Kurian and Mark A. Lamport. *Encyclopedia of Christian Education*. Maryland: Rowman & Littlefield, 2015, 595-97.

Payne, D.F. "Education." Edited by J.D. Douglas. *The New Bible Dictionary*. Grand Rapids: WM B. Eerdmans, 1979, 335-37.

Ryken, Leland, James C. Wilhoit, and Tremper Longman III, eds. "Teacher, Teaching." *Dictionary of Biblical Imagery*. Downers Grove: InterVarsity Press, 1998, 842-44.

Stonehouse, Catherine. "Moral Development." *Evangelical Dictionary of Christian Education*. Grand Rapids: Baker Books, 2002, 484-88.

West, Barbara A. "Dravidian." *Encyclopaedia of the Peoples of Asia and Oceania*. New York: Infobase Publishers, 2010, 193-94.

Winchester, B.S. "Religious Education, Aims of." Edited by John T. McFarland, B.S. Winchester, Douglas R. Fraser, and J. Williams Butcher. *The Encyclopaedia of Sunday Schools and Religious Education*. New York: Thomas Nelson & Sons, 1915, 890-96.

Online Sources

"About Us." *Southern Methodist Church in India, Official Website*. http://www.southernmethodistchurch.in/. Accessed September 28, 2016.

Altman, Dale Linder. "SMC President Visits Churches in India." *The Times and Democrat*. September 15, 2013.

http://thetandd.com/lifestyles/magazine/smc-president-visits-churches-in-india/article_9de49248-1cdd-11e3-b280-0019bb2963f4.html. Accessed September 28, 2016.

"Andhra Pradesh State Profile." PDF. *National Institute of Disaster Management*, http://nidm.gov.in/PDF/DP/ANDHRA.pdf. Accessed September 14, 2016.

Cabral, Hannibal. "Mission in the Context of Plurality." *World Council of Churches*. http://wcc-coe.org/wcc/what/interreligious/cd32-05.html. Accessed June 13, 2016.

"Congregations." *Merrian Webster Online Dictionary*. http://www.merriam-webster.com/dictionary/congregations. Accessed September 16, 2015.

"Economic Development of Telangana." *Agricultural Department of Telangana*, http://agri.ap.nic.in/. Accessed September 16, 2016.

"Economy of Andhra Pradesh." PDF. *Andhra Pradesh State Portal Official*, http://www.ap.gov.in/AP%20State%20Statistical%20Abstract%20May%202014/4_AP_Economy.pdf. Accessed September 16, 2016.

"History of Southern Methodist Church." *The Southern Methodist Church, Official Website*. thesmc.org/aboutus.html. Accessed October 31, 2016.

"Holism." *English Oxford Living Dictionaries*. https://en.oxforddictionaries.com/definition/holism. Accessed November 4, 2016.

"Holistic Education: An Introduction, Page 3." *Holistic Education*. http://www.holistic-education.net/visitors3.htm. Accessed January 23, 2017.

"India's Richest." *Forbes.com*, http://www.forbes.com/lists/2010/77/india-rich-10_Indias-Richest_Rank.html. Accessed September 16, 2016.

Jain, Bharti. "Nearly 60% of Indians Speak a Language Other than Hindi." *The Times of India*. June 21, 2014, Delhi edition.

http://timesofindia.indiatimes.com/india/Nearly-60-of-Indians-speak-a-language-other-than-Hindi/articleshow/36922157.cms. Accessed September 14, 2016.

"Language and Culture." *Telangana State Portal Official*, http://www.telangana.gov.in/About/Language. Accessed September 16, 2016.

Moffitt, Bob. "The Role of the Church." In *Holistic Mission*. Pattaya, Thailand: Lausanne Committee for World Evangelization, 2004. https://www.lausanne.org/wp-content/uploads/2007/06/LOP33_IG4.pdf. Accessed November 11, 2016.

Patil, Bal. "NATIONAL MINORITY STATUS FOR JAIN COMMUNITY IN INDIA." *The India Post*, July 11, 2008, sec.

Religion. http://www.theindiapost.com/articles/national-minority-status-for-jain-community-in-india/. Accessed November 1, 2016.

Pilli, Joshua. "UECF History." *United Evangelical Christian Fellowship*. http://www.uecf.net/history.htm. Accessed November 1, 2016.

"Population by Religious Community." 2011 CENSUS. *Government of India: Ministry of Home Affairs*, http://www.censusindia.gov.in/2011census/C-01.html. Accessed September 19, 2016.

"Profile of Telangana." *Telangana Online*, http://www.telanganaonline.in/About/Profile/index.html. Accessed September 14, 2016.

"Special Economic Zones of Andhra Pradesh." PDF. *SEZ India*, https://web.archive.org/web/20091007035200/http://www.sezindia.nic.in/HTMLS/578FormalapprovalsgrantedunderSEZAct19thJune,09.pdf. Accessed September 16, 2016.

"The Holy Spirit as Teacher." *Knowing Jesus*. Accessed November 11, 2016. http://bible.knowing-jesus.com/topics/The-Holy-Spirit-As-Teacher.

"Transformation." *Merrian Webster Online Dictionary*. http://www.merriam-webster.com/dictionary/transformation. Accessed September 16, 2015.

Webster, Noah. "Noah Webster Quotes." *Brainy Quote*, http://www.brainyquote.com/quotes/quotes/n/noahwebste394286.html. Accessed September 13, 2016.

Thesis and Paper Presentations

Matshiga, Dumile Johannes. "Christian Education in the Baptist Convention of South Africa with Special Reference to Churches in the Transvaal: A Practical Theological Investigation." PhD Dissertation, University of Pretoria, 2001.

Roxas, Noel S. "Transformation." presented at the Integrated Paper Presentation, Manila, November 8, 2014.

Appendix I - Maps

Maps of Telangana & Andhra Pradesh

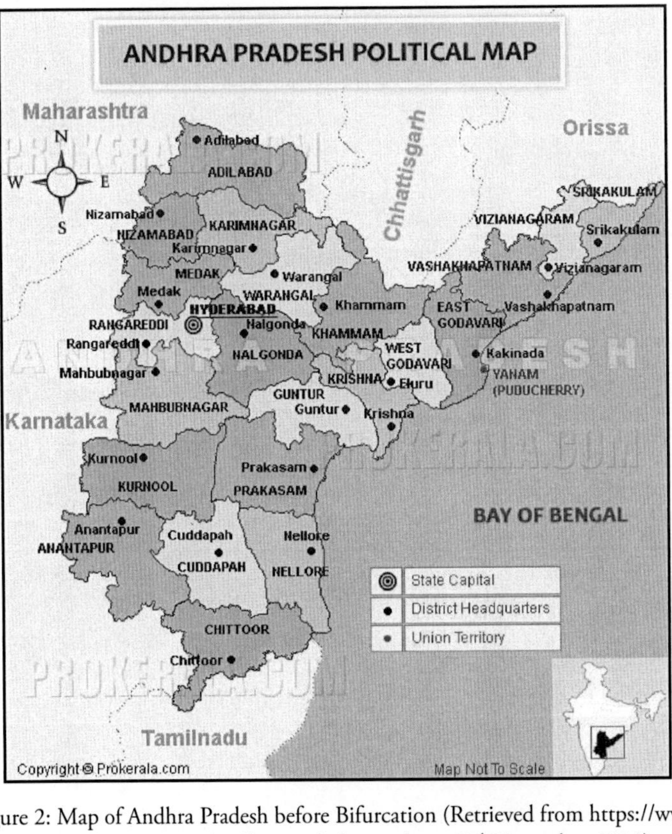

Figure 2: Map of Andhra Pradesh before Bifurcation (Retrieved from https://www.prokerala.com/maps/andhra-pradesh-map.htm, 27th November, 2018)

Figure 3: Map of Telangana State after Bifurcation of Andhra Pradesh (Retrieved from Maps of India, 27th November, 2018)

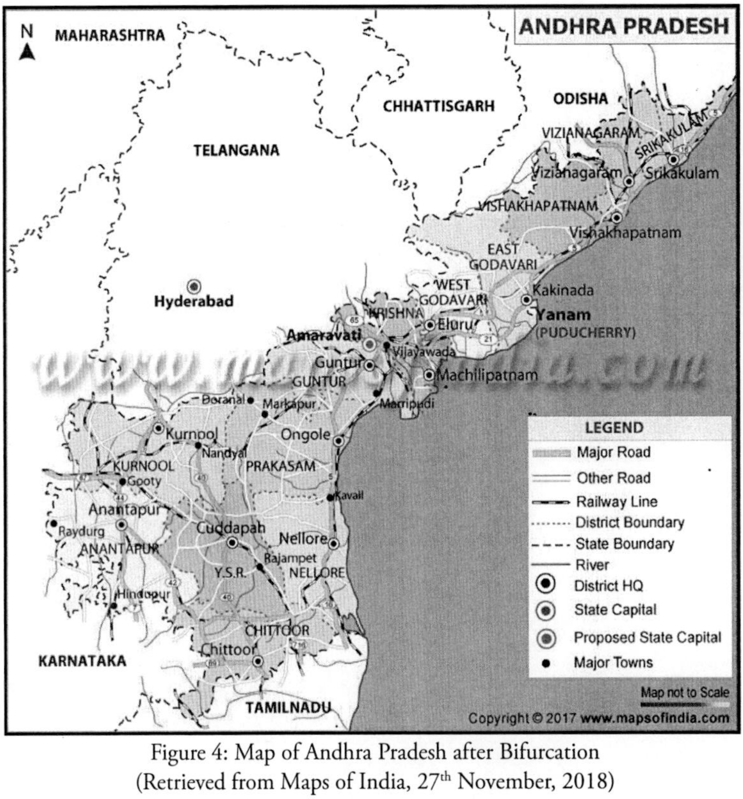

Figure 4: Map of Andhra Pradesh after Bifurcation
(Retrieved from Maps of India, 27th November, 2018)